AROUND & ABOUT The SMUGGLERS' WAYS

DAVID MUDD

BOSSINEY BOOKS

ACKNOWLEDGEMENTS

THE author is grateful to Her Majesty The Queen for her gracious permission to reproduce a portrait of a corporal in the Dragoons.

He would also like to thank Mr David Rankin-Hunt, of the Royal Collection, for his assistance; Mr Cairns Boston, managing director, Land's End Limited, for permission to take photographs of the tableaux at the Last Labyrinth; Mr Eric Bradshaw, of Camborne, a descendant of Henry Cuttance, for the loan of the rare Charles Dickens volume *All the Year Round*; Mr Martin Dennis, of HM Customs & Excise Museum and Exhibition; Mr Gilbert Denton, archivist of H.M. Customs & Excise, for his assistance in obtaining access to restricted publications and departmental records; Mr David Ivall, assistant archivist, Cornwall Record Office, despite his wise observation that smugglers 'tended not to keep written records'; the House of Commons library; the research library of the Royal Institution of Cornwall; and his wife, Diana, for many of the photographs and drawings.

He also wishes to express his gratitude for the enthusiasm, encouragement, guidance and professionalism of Michael Williams and the entire Bossiney Books team as well as to the printers, the booksellers . . . and the readers (preferably those who have bought his book, rather than those who have borrowed copies from someone else).

FRONT COVER PHOTOGRAPH: RAY BISHOP

PHOTOGRAPHS: RAY BISHOP; DAVID MUDD; DIANA MUDD; HERBERT HUGHES.

DRAWINGS: W. DANIEL; DIANA MUDD; W. PENALUNA; THOMAS ROWLANDSON; WILLIAM WALLACE; W. WESTALL.

SPECIAL ILLUSTRATIONS: Page 38 (lower), by Gracious Permission of Her Majesty the Queen; Pages 14, 52, 69 and back cover, Pyne and Natts, courtesy of HM Customs & Excise Museum; pages 10 and 21 (upper), HM Customs & Excise Museum; pages 18, 26 (lower) 87 and 93, Courtesy The Last labyrinth, Land's End.

First published 1991 by Bossiney Books, St Teath, Bodmin, Cornwall.
Typeset and printed by Penwell Print Ltd, Callington, Cornwall.

© David Mudd

ISBN 0948158 70 0

ABOUT THE AUTHOR – AND THE BOOK

DAVID MUDD's love of Cornwall and all things Cornish goes without saying. Born in Falmouth, in 1933, most of his life has been spent either writing about his beloved county as a journalist; describing its features and perversities as a radio and television journalist; talking about it to Cornish exiles overseas whenever he gets the chance; fighting for its people, its industries and its way of life as Member of Parliament for Falmouth and Camborne since June 1970; or writing of its social history and curiosities in his thirteen solo and four jointly-written books to date.

As befits someone coming from a long line of seafarers on both sides of his family, he has served in the Merchant Navy on the famous Union-Castle liners linking Southampton with South Africa. As he says: 'The sea is so much in my blood that I am sure there is a thirteenth sign of the zodiac – Spinnaker – that characterises all those with brine rather than blood in their veins, and who have shared the privilege of the Ancient Mariner's skill for telling a compelling yarn'.

In his work as a Member of Parliament he has, in the United Kingdom and the Far East, come across Customs and Excise in its many roles, as well as having met smugglers. Welcoming the chance to turn the spotlight on the 'industry' in Cornwall, David says the word pictures he has tried to present have been immensely helped by the enthusiasm and skill of his wife, Diana, who has contributed some of the many photographs and diagrams so vital to his book.

SETTING THE SCENE

ALTHOUGH modern Customs and Excise activity in Cornwall can involve capturing drugs with a street value – in just one consignment – as high as the proceeds from a decade of smuggling in the old days; or the routine collection of excise duty for locally-brewed beers; or checking the tanks of vehicles to make sure they have duty-paid diesel in them, the feeling of the living presence of smuggling has outlived the passage of more than one hundred and fifty years since the last conviction for 'traditional' smuggling.

Sit in the bar at the *Ship*, at Porthleven, the *Sloop*, at St. Ives, or the *Smuggler*, at Cawsand, on a winter's night and history comes to life. The rain lashes down outside, the fire roars; the conversation is discreet and subdued; and eyes turn instinctively towards the door whenever it opens to admit a newcomer.

In the great and colourful days of smuggling, Cornwall's pubs held a colourful collection of some of the less attractive members of society. There would be the smuggler and some of his crew; the merchant who would buy or arrange shipments; the informer who might tell the smugglers of some forthcoming Customs or Coastguard operation; or the undercover agent listening to every fragment of conversation in the hope it would lead to an arrest and a seizure of contraband.

There would be the stool-pigeon willing to assist either side against each other; and the customers who were delighted to buy cut-price spirits, tobacco, tea or coffee.

If the door burst open and someone dashed in to cry 'e's dead', conversation would stop to await further details of whether the victim was an Excise officer or a smuggler. Reactions would be contradictory. Far from greeting the news of an officer's death, many smugglers would be inclined towards sadness out of genuine regret at the loss of life. Others, although tempted to rejoice, would be fearful as to the extra activity in the community as every possible step would be taken to trace the culprits.

Similarly, the law officers would regard the death of a smuggler with a mixture of caution and relief. Were he a known man of violence, then the world were well rid of him. If, however, he were the victim of excessive zeal and incompetence, the community would unite against the forces of Customs and Excise and even informers would remain silent.

For much of the time, though, the two hundred year 'war' between Cornish smugglers and the Revenue was fought with mutual respect. There were no rules of war, but there could be give and take on both sides in the knowledge that destroying a fragile and unwritten balance could lead to horrendous repercussions against officers, communities and people alike.

It is, indeed, only a short step in time between many Cornish pubs of today and their customers of the past. It's a step easily covered without too much imagination. The lights are still dim; the storm still rages outside; the beer and spirits still flow; tobacco still clouds the air in wreaths of aromatic smoke; and heads still turn, and conversation drops to a lower volume as a stranger enters . . .

WHERE TALES ARE TOLD ... St Ives, little changed today from the way it looked in 1860.

THE SLOOP INN in the town, haven yet for fishermen and a place where visitors gather to hear the salty yarns still passed down the generations.

Chapter One

'No more barbarous murder was ever committed'

CHRISTMAS EVE 1822 had brought a very boring patrol to the crew of a Preventive Service boat stationed at St. Ives. There had been even less routine activity than usual and, with thoughts of at least one day ashore with their families, the crew was heading back around Land's End.

Then, with understandably mixed feelings, they came across what was obviously a very large and well-crewed smuggling lugger. Although nobody relished the thought of being killed or wounded in what could be a bloody encounter with desperate men, the Customs crew closed with their quarry and put men on board. One look was enough. She was loaded with kegs of spirits and, even worse, had at least thirty men manning her.

But, unusually, the smugglers had actually allowed the rummage crew to come alongside and had even accepted their lines and made them fast.

As the officer and his crew stepped on board, they were offered a sample of the cargo. As, unsure what to do for the best, they returned to their cutter, they were handed enough spirit to make grog. Then, as the large lugger gathered sail and resumed her voyage, the smugglers wished their usual adversaries a Merry Christmas and a safe journey home!

Drawing a seasonal and charitable veil over what could have led to serious charges of a major breach of duty, the official report noted that *'the smugglers were too numerous to afford the slightest chance of success in a contest, which the crew of the preventive boat very wisely avoided'*.

The fact that the incident was recorded as being so remarkable indicates that the smugglers were not, as Adam Smith had described them, *'persons who, though no doubt highly blamable for violating the laws of this country, are frequently incapable of violating those of natural justice'*, but more in keeping with Dr. Johnson's view that a smuggler was *'a wretch who, in defiance of justice and the laws, imports or exports goods either contraband or without payment of the customs'*.

As the Preventive Service in Cornwall was to prove, smugglers were certainly not otherwise law-abiding folk who would, when challenged, meekly accept arrest or abandon their illegal imports. On the contrary, they would fight, plunder, steal, threaten, stab, shoot, maim or kill if the need arose.

In December 1768, William Odgers, an Excise officer stationed at Porthleven was murdered in what was described – even by the brutal standards of the day – as being *'a most barbarous manner'* after he, and a fellow officer, James Richards, had seized prohibited goods from a group of well-known local villains.

Reporting to the Commissioners of Customs that *'no more barbarous murder was ever committed'*, the Collector at Penzance knew that only a large reward and possible immunity from prosecution for an informer would produce the evidence necessary to get a conviction.

The Commissioners agreed and set a £100 bounty. Information began to trickle in to the authorities. But it wasn't good news.

By the time an inquest had been held, and Melchisideck Kinsman, of Gwennap, had been named as the wanted man, together with unknown accomplices, word had reached the investigators that two of the wanted men had fled to Cherbourg and another two to Morlaix, thus obstructing the coroner's hope that: *'although smugglers are very cautious of speaking against each other, there is great reason to hope that the perpetrators of this horrid act may be brought swiftly to Justice'*.

Intelligence reaching the Customs suggested that the story of the flight to France might have been a

SECRET WAYS … The cobbled streets and narrow alleys of St Ives hid many a smuggler and his contraband in days gone by and provided many an opportunity to outwit the law. It would have been a brave Customs man who walked these streets after dark.

ON PATROL … The waters around the North Cornwall coast were regularly patrolled by the Preventive Service.

red herring and that the wanted men were much nearer home.

In January 1769, they learned that one possible witness against Kinsman, a man named Alexander Hampton, had been offered £300 to get out of Britain and to stay away for two years. But, rumour had it, Hampton was so shocked by what he had seen that he had said he would 'not take the price of blood'.

There was one snag. Although the authorities did not know where Hampton was hiding, Kinsman's cronies did. *'Several times since his refusal the smugglers have threatened his life and appeared armed, surrounding his house. The murderers are seen publicly in the neighbourhood and, it is thought, at night sleep in their usual habitations'*, officials reported.

The Customs asked troops to make a series of simultaneous raids on suspected houses. This approach failed when the soldiers asked whether a magistrate's warrant had any validity if served by the military rather than by the civil power. They requested the written authority of the War Office.

In the meantime, the witness, Hampton, had fled his normal home and was in hiding in Redruth. He contacted the Commissioners and asked for financial support as he could not be seen in public. He was awarded 7s (35p) a week and this was increased to 10s (50p) a few months later.

As time went on without the arrest of Kinsman and his henchmen, Hampton became desperate with fear. *I fear that you have forgot me'*, he wrote to the authorities. *'I am under so many dangers of my life to be taken from me. Since I saw you, they have been about my house and, I am informed, with guns. But God had delivered me in time of trouble. I deserve that you will not forget me. It is your power to be my friend which am brought me and my family almost to poverty. I can't go to get my bread, by reason of the enemy. You know how, Sir I can't hold out any longer without your help. I hope you will be my friend and that God will reward in time'.*

In March 1769, some sixteen months after the murder, Kinsman and his thugs were arrested after *'a terrible conflict in which one was greatly wounded'*, and sent for trial at Cornwall assizes.

The evidence was overwhelming and the judge, the Customs and the court were in little doubt as to the outcome. There was disbelief, horror and frustration, when *'notwithstanding the clearness of the proof, the jury (contrary to the opinion of the judge and to the amazement of the court) returned a verdict of not guilty'*, the Commissioners were told.

Perhaps the jury hadn't been bribed or threatened. But was it just coincidence that three of them disappeared immediately after the verdict had been announced, and one was later seen in a nearby pub drinking with one of Kinsman's friends?

Clashes between smugglers and the Revenue men occurred with frightening regularity. At Marazion, in 1755, the chapel bell rang a merry peal when, on two occasions, large groups of upwards of sixty smugglers were involved in victorious conflict and drove off the law officers.

SMUGGLERS' END ... Launceston Castle where so many criminals ended their days – if not on the gallows, then succumbing to the dreaded gaol fever.

In 1774, a Customs officer, backed by a party of Marines, waylaid a group of smugglers in which one of the latter was killed by a Marine's musket-shot. It came as little surprise when the inquest jury decided that the Marine was guilty of murder, and sent him for trial at the Assizes. The only reason that the luckless man was acquitted was because the Crown prosecutor decided against attending the court as Launceston was currently the centre of an outbreak of severe gaol fever.

Often the smugglers, or their associates, were the target of other criminals. In 1792, for instance, Martha Blewett was killed near Mousehole for the money she was carrying after selling contraband salt to those working in the pilchard-curing trade. Martha was intercepted as she made her way home by a young fisherman, William Trewavas, who cut her throat from ear to ear.

There was no local sympathy or support for him and he was found guilty at Launceston assizes and hanged there just one year after the murder.

Even the innocent traveller could fall victim to zealous Customs officers as much as to smugglers wishing to erase the memory of possible witnesses.

In 1799, a couple of officers mistakenly thought that two travellers between Truro and Bodmin were carrying contraband. They protested their innocence but, as *The Gentleman's Magazine* of 27 June 1799 reported: *'the suspects put up an obdurate resistance, until at length being overpowered by their desperate antagonists they were left dead on the spot. The Excisemen then absconded'*.

Officious zeal, too, cost a young Mylor man his life in 1814. Returning from a fishing trip, he was slow to answer a Customs challenge. The inscription on his grave tells:

> *'We have not a moment we can call our own.*
> *Officious Zeal in luckless hour laid wait*
> *And wilful sent the murderous ball of Fate!*
> *James to his home, which late in health he left,*
> *Wounded returns – of life is soon bereft'*.

Attempting to seize illegal goods from one of two suspects an Exciseman, Richard Pentecost, of St. Keverne, was involved in a scuffle. As he and his adversary fell to the ground, the other man – John Stephens – shot him dead in cold blood, in December 1804.

Five years later, in March 1809, *The Royal Cornwall Gazette* reported the eventual arrest of three men involved in an incident some five years earlier, near Land's End, and in which shots had been fired at Revenue officers. Reported the paper: *'A man called George, involved in the same affair, was executed some time ago on the oath, we are told, of his brother'*.

Britain was rocked when, in May 1812, the then Prime Minister, Spencer Perceval, was shot dead by a mentally-disturbed attacker actually in the House of Commons.

The authorities were therefore particularly worried when the Customs Collector at Falmouth, James Platt, received an anonymous letter from somebody who could obviously not be regarded as being a friend or a member of his fan club!

'Pray to God to forgive you, Joseph Platt, your doom is fixed as Perceval received his death by a ball, so you shall fall. Your late proceedings with the packets has driven me to despair, & ere I leave this earth, my determination is fixed to put an end to your wicked and cruel existance, unless you discontinue your committing such robberies as you and your crew have perpetrated for some time past. I give you, J. Platt, to consider of this as above until 30th March 1813, my Dr. friend although my cruel enemie and my ruien, for the sake of your soul, pray to Jesus to forgive you, I say again your fate is fixed'.

The letter was signed: *'A friend to the community'*.

Whether the letter was serious or a hoax was never established, although the Commissioners of His Majesty's Customs offered a reward of £50 in their hunt for the writer.

If Mr Platt's correspondent was worth only a £50 reward, those who assaulted officers at St. Ives, in

WE HAVE NOT A MOMENT WE CAN CALL OUR OWN

In MEMORY of

THOMAS JAMES

Aged 35 Years

Who on the Evening of the 6 Dec
1814 on his return to Flushing from
St Mawes in a Boat, was Shot by a Cus-
-tom house Officer and Expired in a
few hours after.

Officious zeal in luckless hour essay'd,
And wilful sent the murdrous Ball that fired
JAMES to his home which late in health he left
Wounded retains of life is now bereft

VICTIM OF OFFICIOUS ZEAL … The tombstone of a young fisherman from Mylor who failed to respond quickly enough to a Customs challenge.

November 1815, were four times as valuable with a reward of £200 for the identities of those who had recovered between two hundred and three hundred casks of contraband spirit from one Richard Hosking, and his assistants *'after which they were violently assaulted, and obstructed by a great number of smugglers unknown, who rescued and carried away the said goods'*.

Whether or not the month of November brought a pre-Christmas urgency to the whole scene of evasion and detection can only be open to supposition. However, it was always a very busy period of action and counter-action.

November 1820 saw an ugly incident off Boscastle.

A Revenue crew seized a quantity of rum and spirits and pulled their boat up out of the water and onto the beach so that they could guard the seizure until troops could be summoned to escort it into proper custody.

However, soon afterwards a large smuggling vessel came into sight and dropped anchor off the beach, lowering two boats containing armed men as she did so. They started firing at the men on the beach, the Revenue officers returning fire until their ammunition was exhausted. The smugglers then came ashore and attacked the chief boatman, Sampson Woodcock, and his men until, by superiority of numbers, they made the officers retreat in disarray. Then, using their own boats as well as the six-oared galley beached by the Revenue crew, they calmly reclaimed their spirits, reloaded and sailed away.

In another November battle, near Constantine, two officers unwisely intercepted a large party of men armed with pistols, bludgeons and knives, and attempted to take several horses laden with contraband spirits into custody. Offering a reward of £300 for information leading to a conviction, the Falmouth Collector of Customs stated on the reward notice that: *'after the said officers had so seized the horses and the goods, the smugglers with force and violence rescued the same from them, at the same time feloniously assaulting and ill-treating the said officers, so that the life of one of them is despaired of'.*

Ten days later – in the same month of 1828 – two officers showed great resourcefulness and courage when involved in an incident at Swanpool, near Falmouth.

Mr Prior, the Falmouth Riding Officer, and his Mylor counterpart, Mr English, were carrying out a surveillance operation on some thirty men running contraband spirits. Seeing that the men were preoccupied with their task, Mr Prior acted on a daring plan to take them unawares and, according to *The Royal Cornwall Gazette: 'at first succeeded in throwing the smugglers into confusion. They had actually seized three horses and sixteen tubs of contraband spirit, believing that the smugglers would make no further resistance. They afterwards rallied, however, came upon the officers in a body and, after firing on them which the officers returned, a regular engagement ensued. The smugglers at length rushing upon Mr English, beat him with their clubs until they thought he was dead, succeeded in carrying off the whole of their goods, there being no preventive people on the alert to assist these meritorious officers who had the courage to attack so formidable a party'.*

Mr English, it was later reported, was so severely injured that his life was despaired of.

There was, perhaps, some sense of restoring the balance when, in March 1835, a large group of smugglers at Fowey were taken unawares by a Revenue party. In the ensuing battle, ten smugglers were captured – and several severely wounded – 118 tubs of spirits were captured and the surviving

SAMPLING THE GOODS …
A safe return was cause for cele-
bration before stowing the valu-
able cargo in its final hiding place.

▲ *POLPERRO ... Where an informant went in terror of his life.*

◄ *CAWSAND ... Where a Customs man was slain.*

villains put to undignified flight.

Surely the most ruthless vendetta between law-enforcers and law-breakers in the history of Cornish smuggling began in February 1799, and ran on for several years involving informers, splitting families, and otherwise overshadowing other incidents.

According to *The Sherborne Mercury*, Mr Ambrose Bowden, Sitter of the Cawsand Custom boat was, with four of his men, rowing from Cawsand beach towards Penlee point, having received information that the smuggling cutter *Lottery* was due to land contraband. '*When he got within about one hundred yards some person on board called out and asked what boat that was? Upon which Mr Bowden replied it was a King's boat; upon which some person on board the smuggling vessel called out and said: "Keep off, or I will fire into you". Mr Bowden again said he was a King's boat, and a revenue boat, and dared the people on board to fire. The people fired with guns or blunderbusses at his boat three times, by which Humphrey Glinn, one of Mr Bowden's men on the same boat, was killed. Mr Bowden then took up a musket which he had in his boat, and fired at the other vessel which slipped its cable and sailed away*'.

Mr Bowden turned back to Cawsand where he went on board *H.M.S. Stag*, where the surgeon and his mate examined Humphrey Glinn's body and found that '*the fore part of his skull was shot away, and that he was quite dead*'.

Suspicion fell on six men, Richard Oliver (26); Richard Barrett (32); William Swartman (24); Philip Libby (42); Thomas George (50) and Roger Toms (45) '*all of Polperrow in the County of Cornwall, mariners and lately belonging to a smuggling vessel called the Lottery, (who) stand charged upon oath with being concerned in the wilful murder of Humphrey Glinn, late a boatman belonging to the six-oared boat in the service of the Customs based at Cawsand*'.

There was no doubt that the man who had fired the fatal shot was Thomas Potter, the owner and commander of *Lottery*.

Of those who had been on board at the time, a man named Roger Toms was only too willing to offer, in exchange for a free pardon, to inform on his captain and to be chief prosecution witness at the trial of Potter and his six former shipmates. However, until the case was heard, Toms pleaded for a guarantee of safety from the local smuggling fraternity of Polperro who, not unreasonably, he anticipated mightn't welcome his treachery.

The Customs therefore gave him the unlikely cover of 'enrolling' him into the service, making him a crew-member of a Revenue cutter. However, when the vessel put into Polruan, he was recognised and word sped back to Polperro. Promising his wife that no harm would befall him, they persuaded her to go to Polruan to see him.

As they met, he was grabbed and whisked off to Guernsey to await a ship that would take him to America. By the time he returned, it was argued, any case against Potter would have foundered due to the failure of the key witness to put in an appearance.

However, Toms managed to contact Government agents in Guernsey and was rescued by them. Within weeks he had disappeared again and was rumoured as being held captive by Potter's friends in a guarded cave on the Cornish coast.

Worried that the Glinn case might fail, the Commissioners took the strange step of publicising the names of Oliver, Barrett, Swartman, Libby, George and Toms, saying that – with the exception of Oliver, as the master of *Lottery* at the time of Glinn's murder; and Barrett as a part owner, as well as whoever fired the fatal shot – a gracious pardon and a reward of £200 would be paid to anyone coming forward with strong evidence and information.

This, although obviously designed to win a long-overdue re-appearance from Roger Toms, suggested that either Swartman, Libby or George might be prepared to turn King's evidence.

Of Toms, though, there was still no sign.

THE SHIP INN ... Porthleven's hostelry where the talk would be of contraband and customs men, of mayhem and murder.

Then came the breakthrough. Following the death of Glinn, *Lottery* had become the most sought-after quarry in smuggling circles. Whilst patrolling the South Devon coast, the Revenue cruiser *Hinde* came across a familiar outline. Although the name had been concealed, it was undoubtedly *Lottery*.

The chase began. *Lottery* was fast and had a skilled crew. She kept out of gun range for several hours in a series of manoeuvres. Then, during the night, the wind dropped and left a dead calm. Dawn revealed *Hinde* and *Lottery* stationary within a few hundred yards of each other.

Hinde's commander sent off a boarding party but, as they began to close the distance, *Lottery's* crew put out their long sweep-oars and tried to pull away. Throughout the chase, the smugglers were firing at the cutter. *Hinde's* commander recalled his men. *Lottery* shipped her oars. The wind picked up, they both got under way. The chase started again. The smugglers threw their contraband overboard but, when *Hinde* moved into gunshot range, the chase ended and *Lottery* surrendered.

The sixteen men on board *Lottery* were arrested and told they would be charged with obstructing the King's officers in the execution of their duty. Yet only fifteen men walked off *Lottery* in chains and leg irons.

The sixteenth man was . . . Roger Toms. Not only was he willing to keep his promise to give evidence against Potter but, he said, two of the fifteen men now in custody – Thomas Ventin and

William Searle – had also taken an active role in the original incident in which Humphrey Glinn had been shot.

With Toms now back in preventive security, the hunt began for Thomas Potter. It had always been suspected that he had gone into hiding in Polperro but that, as soon as searchers appeared in the village, he had made his escape. On this occasion the authorities openly marched soldiers away from the port. As the relieved Potter came into the open, he was grabbed by a specially-selected 'snatch squad'.

He was arrested and, in December 1800, two years after Glinn's murder, stood in the dock of the Old Bailey with Ventin and Searle to be confronted by Toms.

Toms told of *Lottery* being discovered whilst unloading contraband; of hearing shots being fired, of the cable being slipped and of *Lottery* heading out to sea. He said that Ventin had prepared to fire swivel guns; that he had heard Searle admit that he had fired; and that he had heard Potter say that he had taken good and careful aim when he had fired and that he was sure he had seen a Customs man go down.

The defence tried to discredit Toms as a witness. Three Cornish worthies spoke of his reputation of being a liar and a thief.

The jury found Potter guilty, but returned not guilty verdicts against Ventin and Searle.

Potter was sentenced to death, it being instructed that his body be afterwards made available to anatomical research.

Toms dared not return to Polperro. It is said that the rhyme: *'Tell tale tit, your tongue shall be slit'* began there. Everyone, including his own family, turned against him. Once more he pleaded with the authorities to protect him. They responded in what might well have been a fitting way, by finding him a tiresome job in the prison service where, he was assured, even his worst enemies would never find him.

They didn't . . . and he died at Newgate, in protective custody, many years later.

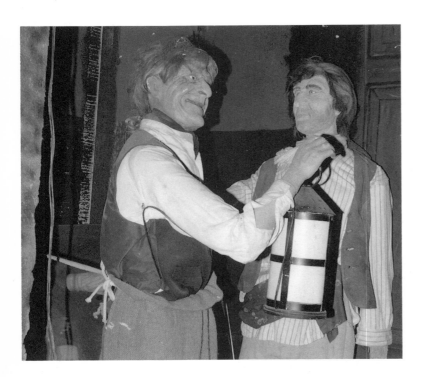

PREPARATIONS … Getting ready for a night's work, lantern lit and lookouts detailed, time now to reveal which cove, which hiding place, is to be the chosen venue.

PORT ISAAC … In 1906 when Herbert Hughes took this picture, a quiet and peaceful place for the children to play – earlier centuries had seen more lawless pursuits.

OLD PENZANCE … Age-old cottages still stand in the coastal town.

Chapter Two

'Twas impossible to resist without a military force'.

IT WAS AS true in those days as it is now. Those in authority, in London, had a strange and touching belief in the tranquillity, the law-abiding nature and the general atmosphere of West Cornwall and of Penzance in particular.

From the Custom House in London, it probably seemed that a man appointed to the post of Collector at Penzance would have one of the most enjoyable ways of life of any officer in His Majesty's Customs.

If, however, the officials in London – particularly the members of the Board of Customs and Excise – took the trouble to read the many reports and requests from Penzance, they would have appreciated that the post and the place were a nightmare rather than a happy and peaceful backwater.

Answering a routine request for a report, in June 1749, the Collector told the Board: *'We beg leave to acquaint your Honours that the smugglers carry on here a greater trade, and more openly run their goods, than ever; and how that the officers here durst not do their duty without being knocked on the head, such are the vast number of smugglers that assemble together, and that, without an armed force, it's but in vain to attempt to apprehend them as we have been frequently acquainting to your Honourable Board'.*

Within three months of painting so violent and worrying a picture, the Collector reported of a wreck, carrying contraband, having been driven ashore at Mounts Bay. The legitimate cargo, of little value, was destroyed *'by the Mobb who came in such number as 'twas impossible to resist without a military force'.*

In an attempt at least to enforce the impounding of the contraband, Excisemen promised to turn a blind eye as long as the wine and spirits were handed over. They were severely reprimanded for their initiative.

Still, even had anything been taken into custody, how long it would have remained secure was always open to doubt.

Red-faced and furious, the Collector notified London, in November 1749: *'Between one and two o'clock this morning, His Majesty's warehouse in this port was broke open and thirteen casks containing 85 gallons of brandy there lying under seizure, carried off. The new locks were tore up and shattered and, had it not been for the family in the house opposite who were alarmed and making some stir, we suppose they would have cleared all those being in the same warehouse, about 130 gallons of Brandy and Geneva but the Rogues, finding they had disturbed their neighbours, made off undiscovered with the above booty'.*

Certainly the news that even more 'liberated' brandy was in circulation worried the Board. Normally contraband was officially sold at a reserved price of 5s 6d (27½p) per gallon. But the glut of spirits literally slopping through the streets of Penzance and Mousehole created a market-figure, in the favour of smuggled goods, at 3s 3d (18p) per gallon.

The Board decided to back the Penzance Collector on this occasion, and offered a reward of ten guineas (£10.50) for information leading to a conviction. Sadly it again lay with the Collector to tell his masters of the facts of life in West Cornwall: *'The reward of Ten Guineas is not sufficient a temptation to get a discovery made. Would Your Honours be as good as to procure a pardon, and also a handsome reward, to any person that should make a discovery such as to bring his accomplices to Justice. We don't doubt but it might prove effective. The Collector had an informer a few days before the seizure was made, against 4 or 5 persons who should be concerned in landing a quantity of prohibited goods and it's very likely they were the same*

The SOUTH PROSPECT of the CUSTOM-HOUSE at LONDON.

from whom the Brandy was seized and, likewise , most reasonable to imagine that they were the persons concerned in the bold attempt of carrying it away. The smugglers never behaved with such insolence than at present, or was it ever known to be carried on with more audaciousness in these parts'.

It seemed an open and shut case. Everyone knew who was involved. With rewards and pardons in the offing, the evidence would be produced. A quick trial . . . and four or five local villains would be on their way to the plantations of America.

Or so it looked.

Sadly, loyalty in Cornwall (or was it fear?) came before duty. The Collector reported, two weeks later, that: *'Having obtained a warrant from one of His Majesty's Justices of the Peace in order to summons the smugglers to appear, who were concerned with running prohibited goods in the Boat lately seized, but the Constables and others excused themselves from doing their Duty in serving the said warrants in saying that the men are already fled. But on the contrary, we are well assured (at this time) they are to be found'.*

SMUGGLERS' HAUNT ...
Penzance had a dubious reputation, its smuggling population ready to use violent means to protect its chosen way of life.

His frustrations grew when, in 1750 he actually managed to get some known smugglers before the court, they having been caught in the act. The justices, John Borlase, Christopher Hawkins and Walter Borlase, dismissed the case. Even worse, the arresting officers had to seek the protection of the court lest they, in turn, be served with writs by the offenders *'who are got to that height they take all opportunity to insult the officers'*. In another incident, two Excisemen were attacked and injured by a smuggler while retrieving a cask of contraband from his home. They were summoned for having entered the house without a warrant!

Almost as bad as ineffectual law-enforcement, the Collector faced the problem of some local officers who were either corrupt or incompetent, or a combination of the two. *'The Porthleven officers are no good'*, he reported to London in 1750. *'One is too old and the other living too far away. The smugglers who, on that coast, carry on almost an uninterrupted trade. We are credibly informed they conceal their goods in the clifts so that, by land, it being impossible to come'*.

Seventeen years later he had to concede the fact that the resident officers on St. Michael's Mount could not be trusted.

Due to the Mount being isolated at many states of the tide, men had to be based there, rather than at Marazion. Questions were asked when it seemed that these men were striking up a rather cosy relationship with the Mount's main trader, a Mr Blewett. After a thorough investigation, the Commissioners of Customs identified certain specific frauds and malpractices due to either *'corruption or extreme negligence'*. Either way, all personnel were instructed to end all social or commercial contacts with Mr Blewett. This was almost impossible as he operated the shops and tavern, as well as being sub-landlord to the two or three hundred residents.

But letters from Penzance were not always loaded with gloom and despair. There were stories of initiative and heroism to report to the Custom House, London. In July 1751, a Penzance officer, posing as a would-be customer, contacted some smugglers in a local hostelry. Wisely, as events proved, he did not go alone.

'Taking with me an Exciseman called William Humphreys, I met with three men, viz . . . Sampson Bramble and John Maddron carrying one cask of liquor, and one John Pengelly, in company with them, with a silver tankard in his hand. The said Humphreys came forward first. I was close with him and put my hand on the goods, and seized it. The said Pengelly then struck William Humphreys with his tankard and cut his head in a vile manner that he was presently in a gore of blood, and struck me off. In the meantime, Sampson Bramble and John Maddron carried off the said goods'.

It was later established that John Maddron had been involved in running 680lbs of tea and 570 gallons of brandy *'and now detected in running 3 casks of rum. He is very assiduous in the practice, to the great prejudice of the revenue'*.

Maddron was eventually arrested, but was discharged from the Quarter Sessions when the main witness for the prosecution, a well-known informer called Thomas Boddily, claimed that when he had made the all-important statement detailing what he had seen Maddron do, he had been *'excessively overcome with liquor and had not been sober for severall days and consequently know not what I had been about; and now Solemnly protest to the contrary to my affidavit; and scarce remember that I ever offered to deposit any such thing'*.

Some cases did result in a conviction despite the threats, the duplicity, the cheating and the lying.

William Allen, of Penzance, must have thanked his lucky stars when he appeared before one of the 'understanding' town magistrates, Walter Borlase, on June 13 1757. The prosecution evidence was admittedly flimsy. Constable Henry Michell testified that when he went to Allen's home, the smuggler fled indoors. *'I followed him and found the door locked. I broke open the door, but Allen had escaped through the window. Hidden behind a chimney in the attic I found a hole. In it I found fifteen bags of tea stolen*

QUIET STREETS … Thatched cottages and folk peacefully going about their business in an era when smuggling was gone but not forgotten.

from the warehouse of His Majesty's Customs'.

Allen argued that he should not be convicted as, in the constable's own words, he had not seen the accused man in the vicinity of the tea at any time. In any case, it could have been planted.

For whatever reason, Mr Borlase did not accept the story. Allen went for trial and was soon on his way to start seven years transportation.

But the general war between Customs and smugglers continued to run in the smugglers' favour. At Marazion, it seemed, they could play off the Customs officers against each other by giving conflicting information whenever it suited them. At Mousehole, the Collector pointed out: *'Measures must be taken soon, or there will be no such thing as an officer to appear out of doors. H. Treluddra had several stones thrown at him while pursuing information, by which he is now confined to bed'.*

Two years later the Collector complained that he could not carry out his duties afloat, as there was no suitable boat in which to intercept, chase, search or arrest suspected vessels. He could not use the boat based at Porthleven which had become *'solely unfit for service, so old and rotten. The boat at St. Michael's Mount is unfit for use until repaired, an estimate of which repairs was sent six months ago. There is no boat at Penzance and the one at Newlyn requires painting and some repairs. Smuggling is carried to great length and in most barefaced and impudent manner on this coast and, sometimes, even under our noses in the Harbour and 'tho' we receive frequent informations of this in the very act, cannot, for want of a boat, go or send near them. When a vessel comes into the Road we have no boat to command to visit her and, as we took the liberty of mentioning in a former letter, the inhabitants that keep boats will never assist us if they suspect her to be a smuggler, as they are all in a link'.*

By 1763, things had reached a frightening level. Realising that informers were afraid to come forward, the Collector suggested a new strategy to the Customs Board. In future, even if men turned out to be hostile witnesses, it would be important at least to get them into the witness box. From then on, as far as Penzance was concerned, every possible line of prosecution would be followed. If reluctant witnesses could be intimidated into saying nothing by the smugglers, they could equally be intimidated into saying something if they were issued with a subpoena, he thought.

Having received approval from London, he proceeded with his first two witness summonses, against two men named Wright and Pentreath. Confiding in his day-book that he might be barking up the wrong tree, he noted: *'They seem shy and I am apprehensive they may step aside, for I'm informed they have said they are sorry that they ever informed against Samuels etc. Not but when they were served last they were ready to go and were here in the office for the purpose. They now both belong to a smuggling boat that has been to France and is now gone there again, and these fellows don't like the name of informer'.*

The ploy succeeded and the number of convictions increased. So, too, did the audacity and the violence of the smugglers. Requesting an extra allocation of firearms including six blunderbusses; twenty assorted pistols; six rifles and twenty swords, the Collector explained: *'As smuggling is carried on in this neighbourhood with great vigour and the Officers of His Majesty's Customs are frequently obstructed in the execution of their duty, we are of the opinion that our having firearms, etc., would be of benefit to the Revenue'.*

The weapons arrived, as did a new boat. The tide began to turn. In 1767 the Admiralty stationed a sloop off Mount's Bay and the 43rd Regiment of Foot arrived to assist. Sadly, the troops were not of much use as, lacking local knowledge, they were often taken in by false information and then went rushing off in one direction, leaving beaches and piers open to the smugglers. The Collector commented: *'I am afraid that great perils now face my officers. The smugglers were daring enough before!'.*

In 1769, the officer commanding the troops complained that the Mayor of Penzance was not providing *'the usual courtesy'* of candles and heating for the soldiers' accommodation. The failure came as no surprise to the hard-pressed and battle-weary Collector. *'It is of no wonderment to me, as he is at present bound over in a considerable sum not to be again guilty of smuggling'.*

The embittered sadness had as much to do with the lack of effectiveness of the troops as it had to do with local 'culture'.

The Collector had fought hard to get military backing. Only a year earlier, in the belief that land-based well-organised reinforcements would drive smuggling from the Penzance area, he had written yet another letter to the Custom House, in London: *'We beg leave to represent to your Honourable Board that smuggling is carried on with such vigour, and the smugglers behave with such uncommon audacity that the officers of the revenue are deterred from properly doing their duty (and more particularly so since one of their brethren was lately murdered in this part by some of these desperate fellows) we therefore humbly pray that your Honours will be pleased to procure a party of soldiers to be quartered here and in the neighbourhood, which will undoubtedly be of the greatest service to the revenue. The last party of soldiers that were here left us the 2 May last and we were in hopes others would have been ordered to succeed them'.*

He suggested that between sixty and seventy men would be sufficient, if stationed at Penzance, Marazion, Newlyn and Mousehole.

It had been a courageous letter for him to write. It was as if he was admitting that, under his control, matters at Penzance had so deteriorated and that the morale of his own men was at such a low ebb that only the arrival of a fresh non-Customs body could regain the initiative.

The troops had come, yet were more worried about candles than captives. Worse was in store. Sensing that there was little love lost between Customs and soldiers, the local people exploited the rift in a very vicious but successful way, by creating mistrust between the two arms of their adversaries.

The officer commanding the 43rd Regiment of Foot wrote to the Collector, Penzance: *'On Monday last, about 4 or 5 o'clock in the evening, Edward Rowling, an Officer in the Customs, called upon us at our quarters and told us that he believes he should soon want our assistance for that there were two boats gone out to take up prohibited goods. We answered that we should be ready at the shortest notice, about 6 o'clock in the same evening. Rowling sent his daughter to inform us that he was going down to the Green and was desirous that we would meet him immediately there, which we complied with. When we joined said Rowling, he took us to a place called the Marlam Rock, saying that this is the place they must land their goods, adding that as the swell of the sea was so great, they could not land at any other place.*

'After waiting there some time, one Richard Pentreath (alias Darlow) and another man, both reputed smugglers, came where we and Rowling were. R. Pentreath came immediately and took Rowling by the hand. They talked together. Some little time thereon, Rowling turned to us and said we had better go away and ordered us from this place, called the Marlam Rock, to the public pier where we imagine no smugglers would ever come to discharge prohibited goods. While we were at the pier, several people passed us with lights and we were apprehensive the smugglers might run their goods at the Marlam Rock while we were at the pier. We mentioned several times that we thought our being at the pier would be of no service and that we had better go and see what the people were about. But Rowling answered it was time enough. Some time after, we saw a boat coming, which we told Rowling of. He answered that was what he wanted. Soon after, two empty boats came into the pier and a great number of people attending them. We leave you, gentlemen, to judge whether it is not likely that Rowling's leaving the Marlam Rock on Pentreath's coming, speaking with him and shaking hands, look as if they understand each other'.

Questioned by his superiors, Rowling denied conspiracy and produced an affidavit from Pentreath stating that he had never given the Customs officer a bribe of any sort, and another statement suggesting that the soldiers had been put up to making a false complaint against Rowling by a group of people in Mousehole who were sympathetic to the smugglers' cause and antagonistic to Officer Rowling. However, as Rowling had previously been suspected of having accepted a bribe *'to stay indoors'* on another occasion, he was discharged from the Customs.

But the damage had been done. The gulf widened. Relations between Customs and the 43rd Regiment became even more strained. And the only people to benefit were the smugglers. The soldiers were withdrawn and villainy resumed.

Writing to the Collector, in 1778, Mr Edward Giddy, of Tredrea, an honest magistrate, spoke of law-abiding citizens having to stand beside the public highway between Penzance and Marazion whenever smugglers wished to use it. Two officers, he said, had managed to get wind of where a sizeable landing of contraband lay concealed in the house of a well-known smuggler.

'They obtained from me a search warrant, but were forcibly hindered from executing it by four men, one armed with a pistol and a large whip, the others with sticks and bludgeons. They were told that if they persisted they would have their brains blown out. As the law now stands, I fear a criminal prosecution would have been useless for the reason, which it shocks me to mention, that a Cornish jury would certainly acquit the smugglers.

'These are facts. It would be mere pedantry to attempt to describe the moral and political consequences of smuggling carried to such a daring height, but I cannot help saying that perjury, drunkenness, idleness, poverty, and contempt of the law, and a universal corruption of manners are, in this neighbourhood, too plainly seen to accompany it'.

At least the Collector was no longer alone in his views!

POLPERRO ... One man held the village in his grip, families dependent on him for jobs, houses, loans and favours.

HIDEAWAY ... A cellar could conceal much from prying eyes.

Chapter Three

'They did great mischief to your Government'

FOR ONCE it doesn't matter where or when it happened. The night was dark. The stranger, walking along the shoreline, spotted a lantern being held aloft. As he moved towards it, he became aware that there were other people on the beach and that they seemed to be dragging heavy casks to waiting ponies.

The truth of what he was seeing struck him.

Going up to one of the men, he asked: 'Where's the magistrate?'.

'Havin' dinner with the captain of Dragoons six mile' away'.

'And where's the doctor?'.

'Staying home tonight, 'case 'e's needed'.

'Very well then, where's the minister?'.

'He's the one holding the lamp'.

As a story, it probably owed its origins more to a joke in a local pub than it did to the spot on the North Cornish coast where it was supposed to have happened. But, joke or not, it still was a tale that told a great deal. For smuggling ran completely across social barriers, local responsibility and any of the million and one differences of value or even of law-awareness that would normally separate law-enforcer from law-breaker; priest from sinner; and rich man from pauper.

Contraband would be hidden in mansion or in manse; in cave or in cellar; in bedroom or in bell-tower; in chapel or in church. So well organised was the chain of smuggling that, even were the Customs to eliminate one link, the survivors would re-establish that which had been lost.

Contrary to popular belief, the 'art of smuggling' had far more serious implications than merely being a harmless spot of adventure that, at worst, raised a couple of upturned fingers against unpopular and high duties on imported goods, or against what were regarded as harsh laws designed to suppress the free-trading nature of man's spirit.

Indeed, had Napoleon said a few years earlier what he said after his capture and during his banishment to Elba, smuggling might have extinguished itself through embarrassed patriotism. Writing of the smugglers, he admitted: *'They did great mischief to your Government. During the war all the information I received from England came through the smugglers. They are people who have courage and ability to do anything for money . . . I had every information I wanted from them. They brought over newspapers and despatches from the spies that we had in London. They took over spies from France, landed and kept them in their houses for some days, dispersed them all over the country and brought them back when wanted. They assisted French prisoners to escape from England'.*

Certainly, had the smuggling industry realised how it was being exploited by the French, the chances are that it might have been a little more circumspect in its range of activities.

It will never be known just how much illegally imported tea, tobacco, silk and spirits passed through Cornwall, or just how many men were involved in the trade. An observer in 1800 reckoned that more brandy and rum was smuggled ashore in the South-West than was legally imported through the port of London, and that upwards of 40,000 men played some part or another in running contraband in Cornwall, Devon, Somerset and Dorset. Figures could not, in any case, be accurate as smugglers did not keep account books, staff lists or payslips. Additionally, Devon smugglers often purchased Cornish-built boats while their Cornish counterparts might operate out of the Devon ports.

But, taking just the small Cornish port of Polperro, it was recorded that smuggling was the main local industry. *'All joined in it; the smith left his forge, and the husbandman his plough; even women and children turned out to assist in the unlawful traffic . . . Lusty seamen these, bearing no malice even when the revenue men scored a point . . . If the seamen were not fighting with the enemies of England they were fighting with its law'.*

Whilst it was true that the bored sons of the local gentry often made runs for little more than the excitement of the trade, the actual operation brought together a wide range of interests and expertise in a team which, although close-knit, was so protected both by loyalty and secrecy that few members of the 'family' even knew, or suspected, the identities of their fellows.

At the top of the tree came the head of the syndicate. More often than not he was an otherwise-respected pillar of society – perhaps the squire, the magistrate, the doctor or the banker. One group, in fact, comprised supporters of both the Church of England and the Methodists. Indeed, so deep did the link between Methodism and smuggling run that when John Wesley visited St. Ives, in 1753, he was horrified to find *an accursed thing among them (his followers): well nigh one or all bought or sold uncustomed goods. I therefore delayed speaking to any more 'til I had met them all together. This I did in the evening, and told them plain either they must put this abomination away, or they would see my face no more'.*

The 'leader' or 'master' smuggler headed the operation. He owned or chartered the vessels to be used and selected the crew. He arranged with French traders where and when the shipments would be ready for collection or transfer. He sold the goods, paid the men and often looked after their savings and welfare needs as well, out of the profits of the venture.

If the run succeeded, he made a good profit. If it failed, then all he lost was his money, since he had usually covered his tracks so well that even if suspicion was turned against him, there was seldom any proof. Indeed, if he treated the rest of his team with consideration and honesty, it was unlikely that anyone would inform against him since, were he convicted, a very useful community friend would be lost.

Then came the crews of the smuggling luggers. Almost without exception they were outstanding seamen with a phenomenal knowledge of the wind and the tide, as well as of the precision navigation that could establish a rendezvous or a landing without the type of error that could be costly in time and dangerous in its risk of discovery and capture.

The key man on the beach was the 'Lander'. He undertook the unloading and distribution of the contraband and the hiring and availability of the necessary man and hoof-power in terms of horses, ponies, waggons and hiding-places.

As one of the greatest risks was that of being ambushed by the Customs with contraband still lying between boat and transport, 'Batsmen' were used to provide a human wall between goods and would-be assailants. They were armed with swords, cudgels and firearms.

Those involved in the landing operation were usually paid at a flat rate of 1s (5p) per night, plus a 5s (25p) bonus once the goods had been transported and concealed. To make their ponies more difficult to catch or hold, the manes and tails were often cut away, and the animals rubbed all over with grease or soap.

Captain H.N. Shore, the great authority on Customs history, painted a slightly different picture of the smuggling 'firm'. He wrote: *'The master-smugglers contract for the goods abroad, or with the master of a cutter that fetches them, for a quantity of teas (called "dry goods") and brandies, and the captain of the cutter*

BOAT TALK ... Old and young engage in earnest discussion about the boats large and small which crowd the harbour. Herbert Hughes took this picture of Mevagissey in 1909. ▶

fixes a time and a place where he desires to land and seldom, or never, fails, being pretty punctual as to the time, if the weather permits, as the master-smugglers cannot fetch all the goods themselves, so they hire men who they call "riders", and they allow each man a guinea (£1.05p) a journey, and bear all expenses of eating and drinking, and horse, and an allowance of a dollop (40lb weight) of tea.

'They always make one journey, sometimes two and sometimes three a week, which is indeed such a temptation that very few people in the country can withstand, and which has been the cause of so many turning'.

Some idea of response to the temptation may be gained from the report, in 1775, that it was not unusual, at Newquay, for the smugglers to have one hundred horses on hand every day of the week, including Sundays and holidays, to spirit the contraband quickly into hiding.

To guard against the remote possibility of any of the beach-porters or riders being in the pay of the Customs, they were only given a few hours' warning of where and when the run would be coming ashore. They would meet some miles from the target beach and then remain concealed in barns and outhouses until, with the scheduled time fast approaching, they would be led to the beach or landing-stage where the cargo would soon be unloaded.

It would seem that even women played their part in clandestine operations. In 1799, when he was going towards Kingsand, the Reverend George Lipscombe encountered: *'several females, whose appearance was so grotesque and extraordinary, that I could not imagine in what manner they had contrived to alter their natural shapes so completely; till, upon enquiry, we found that they were smugglers of spirituous liquors; which they were at that time conveying from their Cutter to Plymouth, by means of bladders fastened under their petticoats; and, indeed, they were so heavily laden, that it was with great apparent difficulty they waddled along'.*

It may seem strange that the women were so seemingly unconcerned about whether or not their grotesque appearance might cause even the least observant Revenue officer to stop and question them. In fact, the rewards of smuggling were so great that it was often worthwhile taking a risk on the proven economics that a team could afford to lose two shipments in three, yet still make a profit if they could sell the third. The profit was related to the very high levels of duty that were imposed on legally-imported commodities.

Tea, for instance, carried a duty of 4s (20p) per pound in 1740. It was already a universal drink from cottage to castle. It could be bought in Holland for 2s (10p) per pound and sold for 5s (25p) per

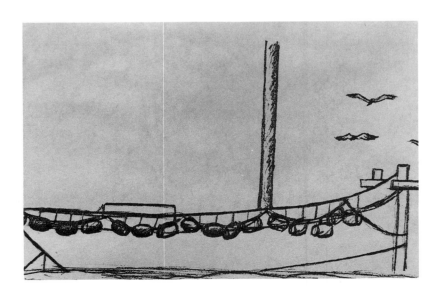

QUICK RELEASE ... Casks slung along the side of a boat for swift sinking should the need arise.

pound in Cornwall, providing a bargain for the customer and a good profit for the free-trader. Four gallons of brandy cost 16s (80p) in France but, with duty added, cost at least four times as much when sold legally in England. Therefore brandy, rum, port, sherry and tobacco, if bought at a quarter of the British price and sold at half or two-thirds the official duty-added price meant a steady demand.

Indeed, the profit – and pay – from smuggling were so good that farmers had to increase the wages of their labourers to keep them off the beaches at night-time and working the fields in daylight.

Not all the contraband had its origins in France or Holland. Some came from greater distances, on board the graceful vessels of the Honourable East India Company when, once the official cargo of teas had been loaded, officers and crews carried out a little private enterprise with loadings of their own. As the East Indiamen made their way up the Cornish coast, they would be approached by Cornishmen in fast luggers who would negotiate a deal.

When one East Indiaman – *Plassey* – was coming home in 1769 she had to play cat and mouse with both a smuggling lugger and with a Revenue cruiser that tried to get near enough to investigate what was going on. The better seamanship of the lugger's crew won the day and, after a bit of brisk trading, sixty-eight chests of tea changed ship. What was particularly interesting, underlining the 'integrity' of the smugglers, was that the shipment was paid for by a cheque for £1,224 drawn on a highly reputable London bank!

In addition to the cheque, the smugglers paid crew members a further £840 in cash in a series of small private purchases.

Selling goods in this way was undoubtedly attractive to seamen on the last leg of their homeward voyage at a time when even their captain was only paid the princely sum of £12 monthly.

On another occasion, private ventures by the crew of three other East Indiamen lying off Falmouth cleared £20,000 worth in China tea, arrack and linens without a penny being paid to the Customs.

After the worries of the Napoleonic wars had ended, Revenue operations led to a change of pattern in smuggling. Beach ambushes, better intelligence sources, more manpower and a variety of other factors meant that it was no longer safe or easy merely to run a vessel onto a quiet beach, or into an isolated cove, and unload directly without the fear of discovery. Even worse, there was the growing reality that expensive and irreplaceable craft might well be intercepted and arrested following a 'drop'.

Something different was required . . . something different was devised. No longer would boatman and landsman meet, thus reducing risk to its lowest possibility.

In the past, casks of brandy had been loaded onto smuggling vessels and already roped together in a way that made it a swift and simple task to sling the containers across a pony's back. Now, by extending the length of the rope, and attaching a stone or a weight in the middle, it was possible to 'suspend' the cargo out of sight beneath the surface and for the smuggling vessel to slip away. Then, perhaps next night, local accomplices would use hooks and grapnels to catch the ropes and either draw them directly ashore or lift them on to smaller boats for landing when the coast was clear.

This took advantage of a new development on the smugglers' side – the constant enrolment of former Revenue men who had either been discharged for dishonesty or, possibly, were attracted to the illicit side of the business because it offered better rewards. Either way, their knowledge of the official mind, and the likely strategy to be employed by Customs and Coastguards in mounting a raid or an ambush, meant that the contraband could stay silently and safely beyond human eyes, although but a few yards from the shore and a few feet beneath the surface while officialdom carried out its predictable searches of otherwise deserted beach and coast.

As an addition to the new methods of delivery, the smuggling vessel would usually leave its berth

MEVAGISSEY 1825 … Boats head for the harbour.

in France or the Channel Islands in early morning, so as to arrive off the Cornish coast in late evening. It would then slip inconspicuously landwards concealed in any incoming fishing fleet or other legitimate vessels sailing in the area.

Once near the selected dropping point, the 'Spotsman' – as an expert navigator was called – would take bearings and cross-bearings on prominent land-points, and the casks would go over the side. In due course details of the 'moorings' would go to the purchaser of the cargo.

Provided it was anchored in a seamanlike manner, the line of tubs would be secure for several weeks at a time. As long as the tub-maker knew his trade, the containers would resist the salt water for a considerable time, thus guaranteeing the quality of the wine or spirits when they were eventually trawled up.

Those who designed and built boats for the smuggling trade had to meet three basic demands. The boat must be fast and seaworthy but, above all, should look as much as possible like similar craft carrying on an honest trade.

Vessels ranged from fifty tons to something approaching the three hundred ton mark. Those built at Mevagissey were renowned for their turn of speed, generated by their sail-area and long bowsprits, and could travel from Cornwall to Roscoff or Cherbourg in eight hours or so. Boatyards at Cawsand and Polperro turned out shallow-draught craft that could work the estuaries, rivers and beaches with ease, either in their own right or as auxiliaries to their larger compatriots. Shallow-draught was an important element of escape as, usually, Revenue ships were cutters carrying a very deep keel and, consequently, unable to get sufficiently close inshore to win the key element of surprise or to engage in hot pursuit along the coast.

Sometimes, though, smugglers actually used ex-Revenue vessels which had either been stolen, or else been sold by tender at the end of their Customs working days.

In addition to turning out some of the finest smuggling craft, Cawsand produced the best crews as well. Arguing for more suitable ships for his own men, the Collector of Customs agreed that: *'The Cawsand smugglers and the smugglers on this coast are all very expert lugger sailors, and will have as many luggers employed in the trade next year (1786) as ever they had, knowing very well a cutter can never catch a lugger where there is room to work their vessels; and I venture to assert they will each of them make a voyage in a week which won't be less than 6000 ankers, or 60000 gallons of spirits; this may appear a large quantity but is nothing in comparison with what is landed in the neighbourhood, taking Mevagissey Bay, St. Austell, Fowey, Looe, Bigbury Bay, etc'.*

His request for extra backing was not only rejected by the Commissioners in London, but they withdrew the Revenue cruiser *Wasp* as well.

Chiding them for their folly, he wrote: *'I do assure you, Sir, she has not her equal for sailing and fitness for the Revenue service. I will mention a proof of the increase in smuggling since* Wasp *has been put out of the service. Spirit, at that time, sold for £2 12s 6d (£2.62½p) per anker; it now sells for £16s (£1.30p) per anker which is less than 3s (15p) a gallon'.*

True to fashion, smugglers always passed the benefit of reduced overheads to their customers!

By the end of the 18th century, cargo-space and speed on smuggling craft were being sacrificed in the interests of defence, with guns and gunpowder taking valuable room. One intelligence report, in 1785, revealed at least five Cornish vessels armed to a worrying degree:

Stagg – Lugger, 90 tons, 30 men, all equipped with side-arms; *Happy-go-Lucky* – Lugger, 80 tons, 35 men, all with side-arms; *Happy-go-Lucky* – Cutter, 100 tons, 14 guns, 30 men; *Glory* – Sloop, 70 tons, 20 men, all with side-arms; *Sweepstakes* – Lugger, 250 tons, 26 guns, 60 men, numerous boats, (each 30-46 ft long) with 10-12 oars.

Various tricks were tried to disguise the smugglers' boats and to confuse the authorities. Some flew flags of other nations, or the emblems and burgees of respectable sailing clubs; others were painted to look like pilot cutters or, in some cases, to look like Revenue vessels. Other captains would carry two or three sets of sails of different colours and slightly different dimensions and designs.

But since, other than at time of war, Revenue cruisers could not board or challenge vessels wearing the French flag, the Cornish sometimes sailed under the Tricolour. Some families, it was said, would send pregnant wives from Cornwall to Roscoff, Morlaix or Cherbourg to win French citizenship for their children.

Against the cleverness and the growing armed strength of the smuggling fraternity, the authorities decided, at last, to increase their operations off Cornwall and to take a higher profile. But, as *The Royal Cornwall Gazette* pointed out rather cuttingly on February 13, 1802, *'A squadron of frigates being ordered to cruise on the Cornish coasts against the smugglers has raised a formidable idea in the public mind of the extent of the illicit trade carried on here. We shall be much surprised, however, if these frigates shall, at the end of twelve months, have seized as much spirits as will be equal to the regular consumption of their crews'.*

In July 1805, just three months before the Battle of Trafalgar, the same newspaper welcomed the idea that vessels seized from smugglers should, instead of being broken up, be used in the battle against smuggling itself: *'It has long been a matter of regret that the vessels which are occasionally taken from the smugglers should be broken up and destroyed. These vessels are in general chef d'ouvres in marine architecture. It is now said Government intends to appropriate a number of them to the use of the sea-fencibles, and that several of these vessels are already fitted up for the purpose'.*

The Navy, it was reported, had found a great difference between the well-designed smuggling vessels and their own to such an extent that it was as if those of the Royal Navy *'resemble the ladies of the last reign, with their toupees and fardingales; while a cutter in the hands of smugglers, who first built them, and who best knew their use, is as unencumbered as a modern belle, and as fleet as the half-naked nymph who out-ran Appollo'*.

The columns of *The Royal Cornwall Gazette* – if, indeed, he ever read them – would have caused little pleasure or amusement to Zephaniah Job.

Born in one of the smuggling ports, St. Agnes, in the 1750s, he had launched a grandiose but unsuccessful scheme to build a replacement harbour for the one destroyed by a storm, at Trevaunance, almost fifty years earlier.

Disappointed by his lack of success, he moved to Polperro in 1774, obviously hoping that a switch of location would mean a change of fortunes and an end to the nagging frustration of having a brain capable of working far in excess of realisable finance.

Arriving at Polperro, he opened a small school and taught mathematics. Sadly for Zephaniah, although the parents wanted their children to know how to add and subtract and do basic navigation, his brand of maths, based more on the arithmetic of construction and civil engineering, drew little support and the school closed.

One of his examination questions ran: *'How many waggons will reach from Fowey to Looe, it being computed 8 miles; allowing 6 yards for the standing of each waggan? And how many seconds are there in 38 solar years? And how many barleycorns be there in 7,842 miles, it being allowed that one barleycorn be one third of an inch?'*.

It was, perhaps, not surprising that the school register showed a growing rate of absenteeism until Job ran out of pupils and finances altogether.

Looking around Polperro, with its whitewashed cottages and its under-fertilized fields, he realised that lime was essential to local needs. However, lime was about the only thing that was not imported by the citizens of Polperro. He therefore opened, near his home at Crumplehorn Mill, a small lime kiln. The experiment paid off and when, in 1806, he lost interest in this form of activity, he had seen the creation of several kilns which, even in those days, made an average profit of £3,000 apiece each year.

Early in 1800 he extended his activities by starting a boat yard and by buying out the only timber business in the district. He could then sell his boat yard vast quantities of wood from his other business and, by adding an extra charge to the boat yard for the administrative and handling charges, create a good profit margin. As Job had a general monopoly of everything that was bought or sold in Polperro, there was no question of his pricing himself out of business or of transactions being lost.

Strangely enough, it was widely recognised that, rather than make a huge profit out of one enterprise or series of transactions, he found it easier to spread his risks and his profits. Admittedly, there was no real risk since his operations had reached such a point that every scrap of food; every drop of drink; every knob of coal; every plank of wood; every flake of lime; every house; every household; every boat; and every business was – to some extent – bound to pass through Job's organisation in one way or another.

He developed his coal business and, in so doing, created the first coal enterprise in Cornwall. He dabbled, too, in corn and linen. His target rate of profit was a modest four per cent on everything that he handled.

Like many of the smaller Cornish villages, Polperro's bricks and mortar was owned by absentee landlords living in other parts of Britain. Persuading landlords and tenants alike that local management was the key to answerability and profits, he contacted the landlords and persuaded them that,

CRUMPLEHORN MILL … Home of an 18th century entrepreneur.

as the man on the spot, he was best suited for the appointment of agent able to set and collect rents. He then saw to it that, as landlord's agent, he was authorised to commission necessary repairs.

Since he also ran a building business, there was no problem when it came to deciding where the repair work should be placed.

By identifying poor buildings and defaulting tenants, he was able to acquire a great deal of property for himself at very favourable prices.

As a public service he drafted correspondence and legal papers for villagers, wrote their letters and ran a welfare service. In this side of his life he habitually either undercharged or else provided a free facility, thus ensuring his popularity on the one hand and an important insight into personal problems and potentially low-investment ventures on the other.

His biggest scheme broke in 1786.

By that time so many Polperro folk owed him so much money that he could have faced an inescapable financial crisis had he been unable to raise at short notice, the massive sums to which he had become committed. At this stage a lesser mortal might have made his excuses and sought an easy escape route.

But not Zephaniah Job.

To cover his debts and his loans, he transferred everything to his latest brainchild – his Fishermens' Bank. He turned aside nobody who sought a loan. He imposed no final repayment date. Within reason, he sought no interest. He was satisfied to allow Polperro to seek deeper and deeper into debt –

as long as it was indebtedness to the Polperro Fishermens' Bank.

His main profit came from the activity generated by his trading terms. If, therefore, Peter wanted to sell to Paul to release himself from the bank's pressure, then Peter contacted the bank. The proceeds would be banked with Zephaniah Job, so he was lender, borrower, beneficiary and holder of security in a deal that could not fail. He was therefore happy to allow borrowing to proceed unchecked.

The more desperate people became, the more likely they became to move into illegal operations. Therefore, through the 'front' of his legitimate role as a dealer in linens, he switched the darker side of his business to the smuggling fraternity. They, he knew only too well, would need money 'up front' to set up smuggling ventures and buy cargoes in France and the Channel Islands. This was, to a man of his business skill, no problem. In the Channel Islands he set up a massive finance organisation that ensured that the money reached France and that the goods reached Cornwall.

For this, he charged a commission of a very modest one half of one per cent at every stage of the operation. However, the year 1792 showed that the pickings were so great – and so safe to himself – that he doubled this to one per cent from loan to collection.

Helping honest Cornishmen to earn was, as he saw it, his duty. However, there were even better pickings to be had. Since no local fisherman could be seen to go from breadline to affluence overnight, he started a service that ranged from banker to stockbroker. He threw in, for nothing, his expertise as a stockbroker and financial consultant in investing the profits of smuggling. That he went for goodwill rather than cash was proved to be a wise choice in that, from 1778-1799 his actual income from smuggling or smugglers totalled a declared £131,000 over twenty-one years, or more than £6,000 a year.

There was only one break in his link from bank to customer, and he filled this when he introduced his own currency notes printed at his home and bank at Crumplehorn Mill.

He was therefore in the unique position that nobody could question his resources or examine the deposits. Thus his bank notes had a credible face value that actually gave them a premium price.

There had to be a set-back.

It came when, in 1807, the Customs decided that Polperro would become their first major division in Cornwall. Pressure on smuggling, plus the ever present worry of being impressed into the Royal Navy could have meant the end of smuggling. Typically, Zephaniah Job responded by safeguarding the interests of those who had given him his great wealth.

He gave away thousands of pounds to families who had either lost their breadwinner or their livelihood.

However, to keep his own interests – and income – alive, he invested in two smuggling luggers, *Swallow* and *Brilliant*.

He died on January 31, 1822, peacefully in bed. When his financial affairs were settled it emerged that, despite the intricacies of his wheeling and dealing on a wide range of interests and clients, he still had more than £19,000 in cash in his home. Could it have been that he lacked faith in the system in which he sought to invest for his clients? Or could it be that, despite the official view that smuggling had been stifled, it was still more active than many people chose to believe?

Chapter Four

'Unbecoming the character of an officer'

CUSTOMS and Excise, although popularly linked as being one body implementing one form of tax, were actually quite distinct in their origin. While Customs was the duty imposed on imported goods, Excise duties involved taxes on home-produced goods. However, as Britain produced its own beers and spirits and fabrics, as well as importing them, the overlap of the two tax branches was so broad that they usually operated as one body, with the Excisemen – in very general terms – looking after the land, and the Customs dealing mainly with the coasts, the beaches, the rivers and the estuaries. It was, however, inevitable that the two sections of the Treasury should operate – and be identified – as His Majesty's Customs, although the words 'Exciseman' or 'Excisemen' were frequently used long after they had officially ceased to exist.

Similarly, although the Customs had its own fleet of generally small vessels, the later growth of the fleet both in size, in type and in scope, led to the term 'Revenue cutters' or 'Revenue cruisers' being applied to Preventive vessels that were still, theoretically, an extended operation of the Royal Navy in support of the civilian Treasury.

To add to the confusion of a civilian Treasury using Admiralty personnel afloat, there was the further procedural twist that, with the approval of the War Office, troops could be called in to assist the tax-collectors.

Clearly there were difficulties, both real and contrived, in which the three independent contributors to a necessary task would either argue or blunder – to the benefit of the smugglers. Equally, the general caution of the troops not to operate without the express authority of the War Office meant that many well- planned operations turned sour or ineffectual when a young and inexperienced Army officer would not allow his men to be used until their role and powers had been defined in writing by Whitehall.

Customs and Excise had been working together since before the days of Samuel Pepys, but they fought impossible odds against a background of lack of manpower, equipment and cash. As the 1600s turned in to the 1700s, Customs and Excise had to maintain patrols around Britain's long and smuggler-welcoming coastline on an annual budget of just £5,000.

Admittedly, smuggling did not become a real threat until the 18th century and, by that time, Customs and Excise had begun to organise themselves into various divisions covering the approaches to the shore; the beaches and landing operations; and the tracking-down of concealed contraband away from the coastline. The small boats used by Customs were supplemented by the Royal Navy and by Revenue cruisers and, in 1713, resources were strengthened when units of Dragoons were stationed along the coast under a general instruction to assist Customs officers in their duties.

However, the forces of the Treasury seemed slow, indecisive and generally incapable of posing a real threat to the contraband-runners and soon became the laughing-stock of the community. Their lack of effect was commented upon in a clause in the will of Philip Hawkins, of Trewithen, who wanted to wipe his smuggling record clear with the authorities after his death. Recognising, in 1738, that *'smuggling is not only prejudicial to the Crown but likewise destructive of the trade of the kingdom'*, he admitted that he had *'offended in that particular'* and instructed his executors to pay £600 to the Commissioners of Customs within six months of his death.

Nobody could ever truly assess the amount of evasion. The House of Lords was told by Lord

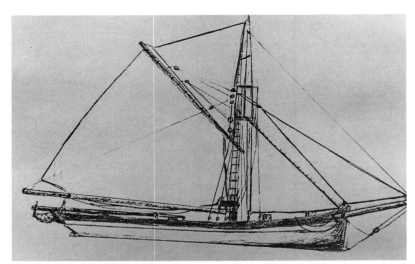

BUILT FOR SPEED ... The sleek lines of the Revenue cutter made her a formidable enemy, able to make good speed through the Cornish waters.

FIGHTING MEN ... Dragoons were stationed all along the coast. Picture by Gracious Permission of Her Majesty the Queen.

Holland, in July 1805, that *'totally to prevent smuggling, all that the legislature can do is to compromise with a crime which, whatever laws may be made to constitute it a high offence, the mind of man can never conceive as at equalling in turpitude those acts which are breaches of clear moral virtues'*.

The Treasury was not prepared to compromise in an illegal operation which, in Falmouth alone, involved goods worth an estimated £4 million a year passing, undeclared, through the port. Falmouth was, however, in a rather unique position in that, until Customs decreed to the contrary, ships of the Falmouth packet fleet were exempt from inspection, thus encouraging a comparatively open market in imported items.

Once more, the inadequacy of the Customs service was a matter of public ridicule, an observer recording, in 1739: *'The Town seems to be in status quo. Trade little, money scarce, a plenty of Smuggled Commodities, and a numerous poor'*.

A state of readiness for expected war with France made it impossible for an impoverished Treasury to think positively about an effective bastion against the massive abuses that were taking place. The need of the Fleet for the ablest seamen, and that of the Army for the pick of the recruits meant that, at best, the Customs service had to do with what was left. Even worse, a Cornishman who could elude Customs could also keep clear of the Press Gang, so the smugglers became virtually an elitist organisation able to operate almost as it saw fit.

However, the eventual end of the period of tension and hostilities changed things in two ways. Firstly, it was no longer necessary to keep the Royal Navy on a full war-time footing. By providing vessels for the growing war against smuggling, the Navy could be sure that its men would be engaged in exciting morale-boosting employment and that cutters, cruisers and sloops operated in conjunction with the Revenue service would be maintained in a state of instant readiness should they be required again against a military foe.

Similarly, the laying-up of ships would have led to massive and unpopular unemployment amongst seafarers, many of whom would undoubtedly have been attracted to the contraband fleet. Therefore, by the creation of a new force – the Coastguard – the ablest, fittest and cleverest would be kept in the service of the Crown.

Thus the Navy reinforced the Revenue service and ran an effective reserve without having to pay for it, the Treasury picking up the bill.

The Coastguard and Customs and Excise came together when, in 1822, the Treasury amalgamated all the enforcement services under one command structure *'consisting of the revenue cruisers, preventive water guard, and riding officers shall be consolidated, and be placed in like manner as the riding officers are at present, under the direction of the Board of Customs'*.

In cautionary vein, the Treasury was disinclined to increase its costs by actually paying for the support services from the Royal Navy and, accordingly, classified them as being 'detached' from the Admiralty for general support duties.

The Riding Officers referred to in the amalgamation were, arguably, the senior branch of the Excise service. Their roots went back to 1698 when, on horseback, they patrolled the coast to prevent the illegal export of goods on which duty had not been paid. On average, each Riding Officer was responsible – single-handed – for surveillance, intelligence-gathering and counter-contraband activities over a four-mile stretch of coast-line.

As they were therefore in constant danger of being outnumbered and overwhelmed, they – uniquely – had the absolute right to call on mounted Dragoons for support.

The coming together of the combined forces meant a massive, but successful, three-tier cordon affecting Cornwall as much as any other part of the United Kingdom. At sea was the Naval presence, or Revenue cutters; then came the Coastguard and, finally, the mounted guard who could raid, pursue or attack smugglers wherever they were discovered.

Integration was of the highest order. Customs vessels were given permission to use their guns to protect British ships from French marauders. The officers were often given Royal Navy rank. The two services worked closely together and, to give officers of the Royal Navy extra authority in certain circumstances, some were authorised to act as Customs officers.

His Majesty's Customs appointed a Collector in each Customs district. Under him came three assistant Collectors, answerable respectively for actions and activities 'On land in Harbour', 'On land along Coast', and 'At Sea'. The 'On land in Harbour' contingent was sub-divided to dealing with ships 'moored alongside Quay' or 'anchored off shore'.

The coast section had, under the assistant Collector, one supervisor and six Riding Officers.

Boatmen could only be recruited if they were between the ages of 20 and 35 and had served at sea, preferably in the Royal Navy, for at least six years.

The efficiency of each district would be the responsibility of a divisional Inspecting Captain who would, amongst other things check on the state of boats and equipment as well as, for the first time, assess all his subordinates on their local knowledge and their awareness and performance of their duties.

Although the idea of the three-tier 'fail safe' cordon was a good one, it was soon found to be flawed as there was too much duplication of duties and responsibilities. Even the Treasury wondered if it was getting value for money when the profit and loss account for the years 1822-1824 emerged.

On the good side, seizures including almost 900 craft of different varieties; 135,000 gallons of brandy; 227,000 gallons of gin; 36,000 packs of playing cards; and 42,000 yards of silk, raised more than £2,825,000 when sold legally at a later date.

But, against the nearly £3m 'earned', came the costs of almost £5m paid in prize money and just over £15m paid in wages and equipment.

The new super-service was, in fact costing roughly six times more than the value of what it was catching!

A review indicated that the recovery rates were much lower than they should be because of the casual relationship, particularly in Cornwall, between Customs officers, Coastguards and smugglers in close-knit communities where some families might have all three 'callings' represented in one household. It was as easy for a Coastguard to pick up strong information about a possible landing as it was for a smuggler to learn of an intended raid or ambush.

Discipline was tightened. Coastguards were expected to live, with their families, in rows of cottages outside the centres of population. To discourage them even from shopping, they were expected to grow their own vegetables and to be generally self-sufficient.

Because of the nature of their job they had to become nocturnal creatures, working throughout the night and resting during the day. Reporting for the sunset muster they would be told, for the first time, of their particular duties or the whereabouts of the observation post or check-point they were to man. Even when in position they were switched at the immediate behest of their superior officer in an attempt to ensure that no smuggler, either by guesswork or by eavesdropping, bribery, threat or blackmail, could anticipate who would be where at any time during the hours of darkness.

This added to the slump in morale which, when coupled with the low pay, led to widespread corruption or disinterest.

Even worse, the gulf grew between the 'detached' Royal Navy senior officers and their civilian counterparts. The touchstone of discontent was the inflexibility of the Navy. Those officers holding Coastguard rank were ordered to wear their non-ceremonial working uniform. However, when on parade, they were expected to fall in on the right of their sections and to salute – Army-style – with

▲ CUSTOMS BOATMAN'S
HAT, 1825

▲ HELPING HAND ... *Implements used for lawful and
unlawful purposes.*

▼ COASTGUARD JACKET, 1820

▼ RIDING OFFICER'S
UNIFORM, 1820

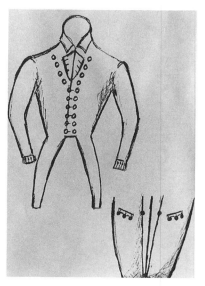

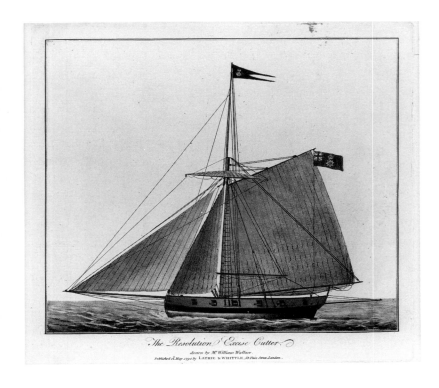

RESOLUTION … An excise cutter drawn by William Wallace. Picture in HM Customs and Excise Museum.

drawn swords. This, they protested, was strictly out of order as their membership of the Senior Service gave them the unquestioned right to salute by doffing their hats.

Additionally, many Naval officers regarded their Coastguard role as beneath their dignity and an infringement of their personal lives and interests. Evidence reached the Coastguard Office, in 1822, that many Chief Officers were so disinterested that they actually concocted duty journals recording events and procedures that had not taken place, *'such conduct being disgraceful and unbecoming the character of an officer'*. In future every entry and every instruction would be signed by the senior officer of the watch, and countersigned by those receiving the orders.

Laxity on the part of Coastguards at Fowey led to at least three successful runs by local smugglers in less than a year. As a disciplinary measure, all promotion was stopped within the Fowey division.

At Looe three Chief Officers in succession were dismissed in the light of suspicion that they had given way to collusion. Although the Coastguards were, in the main, less well armed than the smugglers, they were expected to offer proper resistance if attacked and to withdraw only as a last resort. To retreat from action under any other circumstances gave rise to the suspicion that they had been bribed to offer only token resistance.

The duties became more difficult to carry out. If a man served on a Revenue cutter, he was committed to endless periods afloat, the vessel only allowed to enter harbour briefly to shelter from a storm, take on food and water, or to undergo repairs. At night the cutters made their way landwards and dropped their small boats. As the cutter moved back into an off-coast position, those in the boats would settle down to as many as eight hours of rowing and observing. If the weather worsened during the night, the boat crews had to look after themselves and either ride it out or else try to run ashore for shelter. It was no good arguing that even smugglers wouldn't go out on a stormy night when the lords and masters of H.M. Customs, warm and well-fed in London, decreed that the time of seemingly least risk must be regarded as being that of the highest.

Then, when daylight came, there was another task to be undertaken – the endless 'creeping' for submerged contraband lying suspended under the sea or on the sea's bed. Endlessly, repetitively, stupefyingly, the crew had to row backwards and forwards over a suspected 'drop' area in the hope that their iron grapnels and hooks would engage in the unseen ropes and tubs and bring them to the surface.

The only cheering part of this tedium was that a crew making such a recovery could look towards prize money or other reward for their effort.

Small wonder, then, that Cornwall suffered its share of dismissals from the Coastguard for offences ranging from drunkenness to *'mutinous and most outrageous conduct'* and to desertion. Drunkenness was a hazard of the job, it being a tradition to award a successful crew two or three containers of recovered spirits for what was officially described as being intended to *'afford cheerfulness and buoyancy of spirits'*.

Even if a man lost his job, there was always a place awaiting him on the other side of the fence! James Rowatt, dismissed the Coastguard in 1827, became one of Polperro's most successful smugglers. Two former members of the Revenue cruiser *Rose*, joined the finest smuggling 'firm' in Cawsand, in 1826. A former Chief Boatman, dismissed from the Isle of Wight station in 1830, for refusing to join his crew in trying to put down a riot, also operated out of Cawsand.

Sometimes, though, it worked the other way when smugglers, already rich from the proceeds of contraband, assumed respectability by joining the Customs. One of these, Captain Isaac Cocart, found time to be Mayor of Falmouth twice during his transformation from drink-runner to Customs officer on a Penzance-based Customs cutter.

A third motive for switching sides was that, by joining the anti-smuggling services, the door was opened to the relatively safe acquisition of great rewards through the cancer of corruption with which it was riddled. So widespread was the problem that, even before the final reorganisation could be set in motion, it was necessary for the Commissioners of Customs to proclaim a general amnesty to release Revenue officers from the power, the pocket and the influence of those they were paid to bring to justice.

The final purging of corruption succeeded; the slate was wiped; and those who remained in the service – whatever their deeds or indiscretions of the past – were now fully relieved of the consequences of their former actions and able to dedicate themselves fully to the elimination of the contraband trade in all its forms.

By 1844, the Cornish Revenue force had reached a new level of strength and mobility. The Fowey district had seventy-eight officers and men; Falmouth had been allocated eighty-two; Penzance, forty-nine; the Isles of Scilly, twenty-two; and Fowey, forty-seven. The cruiser, *Fox*, with a crew of twenty-one, was based at Fowey; *Governor*, with eight, at Falmouth; while *Sylvia*, with twenty-nine men, was based at Penzance to cover West Cornwall and the Scillies.

Falmouth had long been regarded as one of the best-run Customs ports, perhaps due to a locally-born Collector, Samuel Pellew, who was appointed to the post in the late 1760s and who acquired no less than half the Revenue fleet allocated to Cornwall in those days. Under his command came *Lark* (twenty men); *Hawk* (eighteen) and the Penryn-based *Lurcher* (thirty). The other Cornish vessels were *Brilliant* (thirty men) and *Dolphin* (twenty-six), both based at St. Ives; and the twenty-five-man *Tamar*, in the Scillies.

When, on the fifth day of his appointment, Pellew found that some of his officers had been involved in helping unload a cargo of illegal wine, at Penryn, he made an example of them and in punishing them, established his own authority as well as setting the uncompromising standards he would expect.

Upton Slip, Falmouth

He proceeded to rule with a rod of iron and was soon feared as much by any of his own black sheep as by the smugglers themselves, but proved that absolute integrity could win respect and results from friend and foe alike.

Once, when anonymous handbills offering a large reward for his assassination were circulated in Falmouth, townspeople – including one or two leading local businessmen suspected of having smuggling contacts – offered an even greater reward for anyone identifying the conspirators.

On another occasion, when dreary and repetitive duties sailing up and down the coastline sapped the morale of his men and led to the resignation of two officers, Pellew and his brother decided to go afloat to see how justified the grievances were. Pellew sailed on board *Lark* with his brother, a Royal Naval officer at home on leave, took temporary command of *Hawk*.

It was April 1786.

Off Mullion they encountered a smuggling lugger. The subsequent report recorded: '*Hawk, being the faster vessel, intercepted her . . . when* Lark *came up, and crossing the smuggler's stern so close as to carry away a spar, raked her with an 18-pounder loaded with grape and cannister, killing the captain and the chief mate, and wounding twelve of the crew; then, ranging alongside, she fired the rest of her broadside into the vessel, which then surrendered. On taking possession, a number of game-cocks were found fighting on the deck, their coops having been destroyed by the cannonading'.*

The prize was escorted into Falmouth, the wounded prisoners being lodged in secure sick quarters, and the able-bodied in Pendennis Castle.

While his fellow Cornish Collectors depended on information gleaned by government agents, spies and informers in Roscoff, Cherbourg and Dunkirk, Pellew developed an intelligence network in Cornwall, thinking that knowledge of the movements and activities of local suspects would be more immediate and more accurately assessed than that from further afield.

This, however, was not without its risks as many would-be self-important people would willingly pass on fragments of information in the hope of winning Pellew's respect.

Sometimes, as *The West Briton* of 9th November 1821 disclosed, this could get more than a little out of hand and become counter-productive.

Under the heading: 'Refutation Of Scandal', the following statement appeared: '*Whereas a report has been injuriously circulated by William Stevens, of Feock, farmer, and Thomas Nicholas, of Truro, solicitor, that I, Charles Elliott, of Loe, in the Parish of Feock, Lieutenant of the Second Veterans Battalion, have laid an information at the Custom House, in the Port of Falmouth, against Thomas Rogers and Thomas Luke, of the aforesaid parish, accusing them of smuggling transactions, I hereby declare the same to be a malicious falsehood'.*

Under Charles Elliott's denial of having informed against Rogers and Luke, came a supporting statement from Samuel Pellew that: '*I, Samuel Pellew, Collector of Customs for the Port of Falmouth, do hereby declare, upon my honour, that I have never received, directly or indirectly, any information from Charles Elliott, of Feock, relating to any smuggling transaction of any kind'.*

This seemed to lay the matter to rest.

But a week later, Stevens and Nicholas plunged the dagger deeper into Elliott's back and, in effect, questioned whether or not he had told the whole truth in his denial and whether, in fact, Mr Pellew had been a little economical with the truth when he had said that nothing had been put to him by Mr Elliott either directly or indirectly.

They wrote: '*A gentleman connected with the Port of Truro, having called on Mr Elliott about some business, the latter said that Mr Rogers had fitted out a boat and gone to Guernsey. What Mr Elliott meant by this statement, or whether he had any meaning at all, other than filling in a few minutes by general chit-chat, it is impossible for us to say; nor is it by any means material to ascertain. The making of such a statement, to one of the principal officers of His Majesty's Customs, who resides within a few miles of Falmouth, was certainly so very like giving information, that we are not surprised if people not used to making very nice distinctions, should see no difference between them – Whether Mr Elliott had any reason for wishing that such information should be acted upon, especially in the case of one of the parties, is a matter that is best known to himself. All we have to say is, that when the commander of the* Fox *cutter did act upon an information of the kind stated, and when he took possession of the boat, in which Mr Luke was, he particularly inquired if Mr Rogers was not on board; and expressed considerable anxiety to secure his person.*

'The undersigned Thomas Nicholas mentioned the circumstances to a tippling gossipper, who quickly raised such a clamour about his friend, Mr Elliott, as induced the latter to apply to Mr Pellew for a lame certificate which he has published'.

Clearly, Mr Elliott had conveyed an item of malicious gossip to the authorities, and Samuel Pellew, anxious to support an unmasked informer, had tried to get him off the hook by doctoring the truth. Sadly, for his own reputation, he was found out both in uttering a fib to cover an informant as well as in attempting to deny that which was obviously undeniable.

The lesson was well-learned and, within one year, Customs officers were more honest and open if found to be in the wrong. Another *West Briton* notice – in February 1822 – was blunt in its apology: *'I, Stephen Bate, of the parish of Breage, Officer of the Customs, having been accused of traducing the characters of William Hosking, of the same place, innkeeper, and Sarah, his wife, do hereby acknowledge and declare that I am unconscious of having done so, but if I have inadvertently cast any reflections upon them, I am sorry for it as I know nothing against the characters of either of them'.*

The gathering of information may have become more sophisticated and more effective. But, on the other side of the coin, people were becoming more aware of their rights against defamation. Small wonder that seasoned Customs men must have thought wistfully of the days when, up to two decades earlier, the best way of getting intelligence was by putting on smocks and dropping into public-houses to listen to conversation between the locals. It may have been rough and ready, but it was less embarrassing if something went wrong.

PENRYN … Where Customs officers and smugglers mixed and mingled.

Chapter Five

'Shewing undaunted courage and resolution in venturing'

WHEN HE was appointed an officer in His Majesty's garrison at St. Mary's, in the Isles of Scilly, Robert Heath probably had little reason to anticipate that the notes and observations he was to record as *'an exact Description of this part of his Majesty's Dominions, how inconsiderable soever it may or has been thought, would be no unacceptable Present to the Public'* would, become one of the most outstanding books of reference on the Scillies, its people and their way of life.

His *'Present to the Public'* was to draw attention to one of the traditional occupations of the islands and the islanders . . . smuggling.

Unlike the Cornish mainland, Scilly could act as a massive transit warehouse for illegally imported goods of every taste, fabric, aroma and alcoholic choice. In a leisurely way, island boats could liaise with French traders or the crews of merchant ships homeward bound; buy or accept contraband; then ferry it ashore and conceal it until it was deemed safe to pass it to those directly involved in the distribution and sale of contraband.

There was, it seemed, no reason for Scillonians to worry about the duty on home-made alcohol since, Robert Heath recorded: *'Here is no Duty or Tax on Malt, and Malt Liquors, which is one Encouragement they have for improving their land'*. Continuing his report, in 1750, he found that: *'The Malt Liquor brew'd in general, has an unpleasant Taste for want of Proper Skill or Management in the Brewing. Yet there are some Families who brew as good Beer as any in England; which shews that the rest might do the same if they use the same Skill and Judgement'*.

But when it came to using that all-important skill and judgement, Robert Heath was forced to admit that it was, perhaps, applied in a direction of which he could, as a king's officer, hardly approve.

For the skill and judgement involved centred on blatant and illegal import operations. Heath was in a dilemma. He either had to drop an important topic out of his book altogether, or draw attention to the flaunting of the law that was going on to such a massive scale that, it seemed, everyone was either a smuggler, related to a smuggler, or gaining direct benefits from smuggling!

Choosing his words carefully, to give as innocent a picture as possible, he wrote: *'Commanders and Passengers of Ships from the West-Indies, or other foreign parts, putting in, never fail of shewing their Liberality, and of leaving some of their commodities and Riches behind them. By this Means the Islanders are supplied with a Stock of Rum, Brandy, Wine, and other foreign Liquors, some for Consumption upon the Islands, and some (by Leave of the Custom-House) for Consumption elsewhere. For the Sake of this Trade, which is their principal Dependance at present, the People of Scilly run very great Hazards in going off with their small Boats to supply themselves from Shipping passing by, shewing undaunted Courage and Resolution, in venturing, when the Seas run Mountains high'*.

So, that was that, there were no smugglers as such – merely courageous and resolute men risking their lives against the elements merely to avoid rejecting the kind gifts of other seafarers, and with the seeming blessing of the local Customs officers.

How true the final point was might seem to be open to suspicion and challenge. However, at least one senior officer was moved to another area when he broke the basic disciplinary rule of not *'inter-marrying with the family of a reputed or notorious smuggler, or lodging in his house, or contracting any improper discipline with him'* when he decided to marry a lady from St. Mary's who came from a long

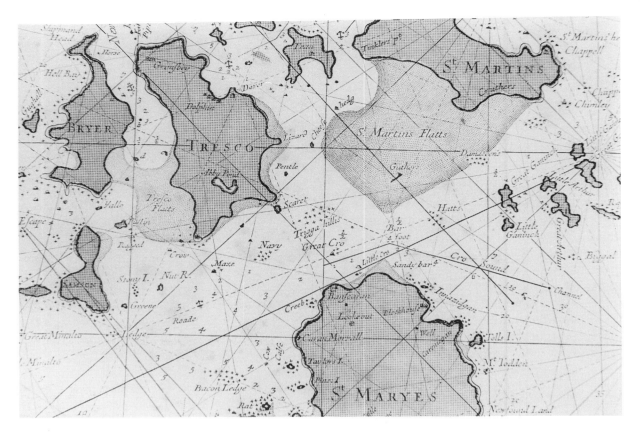

THE ISLES OF SCILLY … In 1756 a world remote from the constraints of the mainland.

line of successful and respected smugglers.

In Scilly, it seemed, as much as on the mainland, it was very much the fact that every man who entered the Coastguard had friends or relatives connected with the trade, even if he had never smuggled on his own account.

The Scillonians had lived most of their lives in the shadow of poverty and, at times, of starvation. It was natural, therefore, that their universal skill as boatmen should lead them to seek the richest harvest of all. It was a harvest that was not seasonal; that flourished when the nights were too dark for anything else; that was virtually an all-weather business that, if anything, was safer in bad conditions; was protected by the coves, beaches, inlets and shoals of the islands; and, above all, had a natural 'cover' in that pilotage and fishing meant that every local vessel afloat had a legitimate reason for being in strange places at strange times and in close contact with every passing ship.

As there was, until the middle of the 19th century, the presence of but one Customs official, it was pretty easy to alternate between outwitting and demoralising him. In any case, since his duties also included those of Receiver of Wreck, most of his time was spent chasing looters rather than trying to trap cunning smugglers. It was suspected that many of the seizures that were made were with the co-operation of his would-be adversaries who thought it better that he should be granted occasional local success rather than seek numerical support from the mainland.

Even if he was successful and seized vast quantities of contraband, there was another practical difficulty, as the Penzance Collector of Customs pointed out in 1761. Regulations laid down that seized goods should be offered for sale by public auction as near as possible to the point of seizure.

This therefore required that anything taken from the Scillonians had to be put up for auction in Scilly. This meant that, as smugglers and bidders were often the same people, the requirement was seen to be yet another bit of government idiocy. Said the Collector, rather ruefully: *'Since smuggling is now so rife in Scilly, we do not dispute the selling. But to whom? None but the smugglers'.*

Even seven Penzance magistrates who visited the islands in 1818, when the battle against contraband was beginning to bite in Scilly, realised that effective law-enforcement could be counter-productive. They ended their report with the reluctant observation that: *'And above all, by the entire suppression of smuggling on these islands (a measure which has been accomplished by the preventive boat system established there) the islanders who had too long and too successfully depended on their contraband trade, are now deprived of their chief means of support'.*

Perhaps certain Scillonians were as adept at acting as they were at smuggling for, far from having seen the art become extinct, they had discovered more successful and sophisticated ways of going about it to such an extent that, in 1828, ten years after 'the entire suppression' the Coastguard and Customs presence had been increased to a total of one officer and twenty-three men, spread between St. Mary's, St. Agnes, St. Martin's and Tresco. And they were far from popular, as the official record book shows with an entry dated 9th September of that year:

'Oliver, the said officer, (with his fourteen-years-old son) went on the landing place to search certain boats. There were several of the islanders assembled, one of whom threw a stone at the officer, and the men threatened him most severely if he would rummage the boats. The officer, in return, threatened that if they continued to pelt him with stones, he would fire among the crowd . . . A man shoved the boat off from the beach, and held up

SAFE AT ANCHOR … New Grynsey Harbour in 1740.

a bottle of spirits, and holding forth the most awful threats if the said officer again attempted to board . . . he seized the officer in his arms (so that he was not able to disengage his pistol), and threw him overboard into the water, and before he could recover himself the boat's crew ran on shore with what contraband goods they had in the boat. The man landed on the beach, seized the boy, and kicked him most severely, the marks of which are quite visible. The officer, also, has been hurted, his watch, commission, arms, etc., wetted, and the pistol lost out of his belt. I therefore humbly beg leave to recommend that the said person may be prosecuted for assaulting the officer, and made an example of to the rest of his colleagues'.

Sadly, Cornelius Oliver lost more than his watch and his pistol in this unpleasant incident. Within one month he had been recommended for transfer to the mainland *'as he appears to be intimidated ever since the assault was committed on him'.*

However, the attack only served to show that, while the Customs operations were succeeding, the point anticipated by the visiting magistrates ten years earlier that 'victory' would create a desperate backlash, had become a dangerous reality.

An official visiting Scilly following the mêlée reported that, although smuggling was apparently in decline, *'the greatest part of the inhabitants are reduced to great distress in consequence, for hitherto it used to be their principal employment, and a strong guard will be always advantageously employed here, otherwise they will smuggle to a great extent'.*

It seems that psychology was then used by both sides.

In 1829, smuggling was resumed with great energy after the rumour had been spread that the very successful and zealous senior local officer of Customs was about to be transferred. Although the rumour was correct, the replacement carried out his duties with even greater enthusiasm and success.

Turning psychology to his own advantage, he spread the word that the interception of two boats working the run from Tresco to Roscoff, *Mary Ann* and *Speedwell*, had been shadowed and eventually ambushed because some of the French smuggling fraternity were not as fond of their Scillonian counterparts as appeared on the surface, and had informed on them.

Suspicion worked and the trade in contraband dwindled so much so that, although in 1831 it was still possible to get foreign spirits, tea and tobacco, it required a few days notice in order that a specific voyage could be organised. Trade and tradition kept things alive for a few more years, but the Scillonians' great days of free trading were in rapid and terminal decline.

FLAG FLYING … St Mary's Garrison, 1740.

Chapter Six

'You could tell their faces as they lay on the bottom'

VIOLENCE was commonplace in the years of embittered conflict between Customs and smugglers. Any suggestion that there was a cosy relationship between the two sides is as false as the frequently-painted picture that, really, there was nothing wrong in running a few tubs of contraband or illegally importing goods in defiance of the laws of the land.

The knowledge that, if detected or detained, the penalties would be very severe indeed, caused the cornered smuggler to fight with ferocity and desperation. Similarly, the realisation that any failure to use the last ounce of courage and energy in any confrontation would lead to disciplinary action meant that Customs officers were not inclined to turn the other cheek when a skirmish looked like getting out of hand.

There was, too, always the fear that even if smugglers appeared to be outnumbered, they would call *'the common people'* to join the fray, thus tipping the numerical balance to horrendous proportions.

When a Porthleven Customs officer tried to take into custody goods that had been thrown ashore from a fleeing smuggling vessel, he was harrassed by the *'gentlemen and common people'* who argued that he had no right to seize anything cast upon the shore. He sought a legal ruling from the Commissioners and was told that anything that had accidentally floated off any ship should be regarded as 'flotsam' and that flotsam should not come within the jurisdiction of H.M. Customs. However, anything thrown overboard, or jettisoned, should be classified as 'jetsam' and be liable for seizure by the Crown.

In October 1791, an official Customs notice drew attention to the size and nature of possible adversaries after the Revenue cutter *Dolphin* had intercepted a large armed smuggling lugger near Padstow. The notice stated that the smugglers had *'feloniously shot at the* Dolphin, *brought her to, and immediately ordered Mr. Osmonde, the mate of the cutter on board, who found her navigated by about fifty men, all armed ready for action, having eight six-pounders mounted, with as many more in the hold, and pierced for eighteen guns'.*

On this occasion, it seems, the smugglers merely reminded Mr Osmonde that he was outnumbered and outgunned were he foolish enough to seek to do battle – and sent him back to *Dolphin*.

The notice went on: *'His Majesty, for the better discovering and bringing to justice the persons concerned in this felony and outrage, is hereby pleased to promise his most gracious Pardon to any one or more of the said offenders who shall discover his or their accomplices there (except the Master of Commander of the said lugger) or the person who actually fired so that one or more of them may be apprehended and convicted of the said offences'.*

In another incident, Customs men interrupted the landing of casks on the coast near Boscastle. The smugglers fled and the Customs hauled their own boat up the beach to guard the booty. A little later, the smuggling lugger returned and her crew started firing at the men on the beach until the ammunition of the law officers ran out. Then a large number of smugglers rowed ashore and forced the Customs men to retreat.

The smugglers not only recovered the cargo, but stole the Customs boat for good measure.

The subsequent notice seeking information about the identity of the perpetrators noted that the *'said smuggling cutter had sixteen black ports, eight of a side, bulwarks painted with a broad yellow side and a narrow black streak above, red counter with yellow moulding, dark gaft foresail, dark foresail, and white jib,*

CUSTOM-HOUSE, LONDON,

14th December, 1814.

WHEREAS it has been represented to the Commissioners of His Majesty's Customs, that on the night of the 7th instant, John Smith, Commander of the HIND cutter, in the service of the Customs, and his crew, when about to take possession of a Smuggling Vessel in the Harbour of Mevagissey, in the County of Cornwall, were feloniously assaulted and obstructed by a large Body of Smugglers armed with Fire-arms and other offensive Weapons, who fired upon the said John Smith, and his crew, and succeeded in conveying the Smuggled Goods on board the said Vessel, on shore.

The Commissioners of His Majesty's Customs, in order to bring to Justice any one or more of the said offenders, are hereby pleased to offer

A REWARD OF
£200

to any Person or Persons who will discover and apprehend, or cause to be discovered and apprehended, the said offenders, to be paid by the Collector of His Majesty's Customs at the port of Falmouth, upon conviction.

By order of the Commissioners,
GEORGE DELAVAUD,
Secretary.

£20 REWARD,

CUSTOM-HOUSE, LONDON,
9th January 1816.

WHEREAS it has been represented to the Commissioners of his Majesty's Customs, That on the Night of the 27th day of December last, a BOAT belonging to the HIND CUTTER, in the Service of the Customs, at the Port of Falmouth, laying at Moorings, at the Green-Bank within the said Port, was wickedly, maliciously, and designedly STOVE by some Person or Persons unknown.

The Commissioners of His Majesty's Customs, in order to bring to Justice, the offender or offenders, are hereby pleased to offer a Reward of

Twenty Pounds.

To any Person or Persons, who shall discover and apprehend, or cause to be discovered and apprehended the Offender or Offenders, to be paid by the Collector of His Majesty's Customs at the Port of Falmouth, upon Conviction.

By order of the Commissioners,
G. DELAVAUD, Secretary.

A PRICE ON THEIR HEADS … The reward for informing on the smuggling gangs was great indeed – but the revenge of the criminals was greatly feared and few dared come forward.

running bow-sprit, and had a topsail yard across'.

Yet, despite this near-photographic description, nobody could recall ever having seen a vessel like her.

The Customs service not only required bravery at sea, but on shore as well.

In March 1830, an officer and four men climbed down the dangerous and vertical cliffs at Hell's Mouth, near Portreath, to surprise men working a landing at what they thought was the safe and unapproachable cove beneath. Sadly, the bravery of the men did not pay off and, in the following few minutes, one had been shot in the thigh and he, and his colleagues, had been overpowered.

Death, too, was a danger faced equally by the smugglers and the Preventive service.

On a January afternoon in 1822, the Boscastle cutter capsized on her way back from a patrol to Bude. In full view of those standing helpless on the cliffs, her crew of five were gradually dragged under the waves and drowned.

A letter written by a returning smuggler, following a particularly rough crossing from France to Fowey said: *'That's true what you say about poor Phil Kingcup being lost. I was coming back from Cherbourg the same night; werry stormy it was, 'though I've seen it wuss, still there was a douce of a kick-up of sea. We was going to start together; but when we got under weigh Phil sung out they wouldn't be ready for another half hour – had to get their tops'l down and stowed. However, after a bit, we'd seed'n following and that was the last was ever see'd of the boat under sail. Next that was heard of her was when she drifted on shore with all her tubs hung round her, and the ballast gone, by Hope Cove. The bodies, four of 'em, was seen lying on the bottom in deep water just outside. I saw 'em mysel'; 'twas the strangest sight I ever see'd, for you could tell their faces as they lay on the bottom, it was that clear'.*

November 1804 saw the loss of a Polperro lugger, overwhelmed by the surf as she tried to enter harbour. Five smugglers, including a local publican, were drowned. Earlier the same year, five smugglers of a crew of seven, lost their lives when their boat capsized while ferrying goods ashore. Reporting the incident, near Stratton, *The Royal Cornwall Gazette* noted that *'the other two were saved, but so much bruised that one of them is since dead and the other is not likely to recover. Most of them were Irishmen.'*

In 1822, *The West Briton* reported: *'The shore of Mounts Bay, near Marazion, presented a melancholy sight yesterday morning. A smuggling vessel was lost on the August Rocks during Wednesday night and all on board perished. The beach was covered with fragments of the wreck and of kegs of spirits. The stern of the vessel has been washed ashore with the words "Rose, James Richards, Gweek", painted upon it. The bodies of two men have been picked up. A watch found upon one is marked "James Gilbert" '.*

Although the newspaper had reported the drowning of smugglers as presenting 'a melancholy sight', the funerals of contraband-runners had a certain air about them bordering on the festive.

The report of a wealthy smuggler's funeral, in 1793, by James Silk Buckingham tells of the coffin being carried by relays of bearers from Falmouth to Breage, with over one hundred mourners following on horseback.

The village inn was used to stage a massive interment dinner, complete with liberal supplies of food, drink and tobacco. On entering the 'reception', everyone was given a large glass of raw brandy. *'These drams were repeated after almost every change of dishes, so that both eating and drinking were more voracious than I had ever witnessed before.'*

When the eating had ended, the mourners settle down with filled pipes, and with bowls of tobacco and jugs of brandy, rum and gin freely available. The church choir then arrived to lead the singing of popular and patriotic songs until well beyond midnight.

There was certainly no shortage of smuggled goods in Cornwall, or of supplies to replace those stolen, seized or abandoned. At Sennen, Joseph Pollard landed three thousand gallons of brandy in

TRESILLIAN CREEK … Such secret backwaters were ideal for smuggling.

one night. In 1804, Customs estimated that seventeen thousand kegs of brandy had been landed at Cawsand and Kingsand alone.

The contraband was hidden in a variety of places before being delivered to its ultimate buyer. At Porth Maer, it was concealed in a cave that led, through a gallery almost one thousand feet long, to Trevemeder Farm. A Padstow farmer hid his purchases under a gatepost; a woman, supposedly in labour, was attended by a 'doctor' who refused Customs officers entry to her spirits-stocked bedroom. A tunnel led from a cave on the beach to the bell-tower at Gunwalloe.

A Preventive officer named White was killed in 1830 when he fell off a plank into a mine shaft at St. Just while searching for concealed goods. Suspicions that, although the crew of a schooner *'conducted themselves in such a careless and unaffected manner as to shake those suspicions'* caused a Falmouth Preventive officer – aptly named Bright – to think that something was amiss. He waited until the schooner's legitimate cargo of coal had been discharged and started to rummage. He was right. A close inspection revealed a false bottom concealing a vast quantity of brandy and gin.

In 1816, four Cadgwith fishermen on their way back from Roscoff with a cargo of spirits found that their destination was to be Algeria and not Cornwall. Intercepted by the Revenue cruise *Hind*, they were carted off to Plymouth, Press Ganged into the Royal Navy, and put on units of Lord Exmouth's fleet of twenty-five ships instructed to bombard Algiers and to put an end to the tradition of the Barbary pirates of seizing British seamen and selling them into slavery.

THE PUB AT FOWEY … The landlord was a leading smuggler.

Cargoes were as varied as the smugglers themselves. When the Commissioners of Customs held a clearance sale of seized goods, at Gweek Custom House, in September 1814, items offered included twelve pairs of silk gloves; four hundred and fifty-two pairs of cotton stockings; one hundred and fifty-three pairs of scissors; three hundred and sixty clasp knives; ninety-five razors; twelve pairs of spectacles; fifteen telescopes; five hundred quills; two hundred and eighty-eight thimbles; and one pound of snuff.

Seizures became more commonplace, but smuggling continued. Polperro and Portwrinkle Preventive boats found a raft drifting off Looe Island, in 1818. Lashed to it was a large quantity of contraband spirits. Patrolling the Truro River, in November 1821, the crew of a Preventive boat saw a vessel ahead of them. They called on her to stop. The crew ran her ashore and scampered across fields to make their escape. On board was a large quantity of smugled spirits.

Penzance Customs officers had notable successes in 1823 and 1826 when they found an illicit cargo hidden under fishing nets on one vessel, and contraband under legitimate cargoes of apples from the Channel Islands on two others. In 1824, two Polperro Customs officers encountered: *'five or six horses laden with small casks, and guarded by several smugglers'*, The West Briton reported. *'Upon which the said officers immediately made towards them, and upon one of them coming up to them, he was struck a violent blow to the head with a stick, by one of the said party of smugglers, but succeeded in seizing and securing from them two casks of foreign rum spirits; that the said smugglers threatened further violence, but on two other officers coming up, they galloped off and made their escape'*.

One of the biggest hauls of contraband tobacco – seven tons – was recorded by the crew of the Revenue cutter *Sylvia*, after a random search of the smack *Kingfisher*, off Land's End. It had been quite a week for *Kingfisher*'s captain. On the Sunday he had been married; on the Monday he loaded contraband. On Tuesday he sailed from Jersey; was arrested on Thursday; and, on Saturday, faced smuggling charges with the possibility of serving a six-month sentence on the prison treadmill at Bodmin.

He might well have claimed to be a victim of fate. But he was as much a hostage of sheer bad luck as he was of fate itself, as *Sylvia* had only approached *Kingfisher* to try to get some much-needed drinking water for the Customs men!

Sometimes, however, the laugh was on the Customs. In January 1831, officers from Bude acting on information received, went on board a fishing boat loaded with suspicious-looking tubs. The crew protested their innocence and told the Preventive men that if they wanted to open them they'd have to do the job themselves. They did – and found themselves knee-deep in decomposing herrings.

PORTWRINKLE … The village pictured in 1825 by W. Daniell.

CHURCH CACHE ... Lelant
Church where smuggled goods
were often concealed.

Almost every cove, it seemed, had its own claim to smuggling notoriety. It is reputed that in the garden of Riviere House, Hayle, there was a secret passage used for goods landed at Godrevy; that Lelant church was used for concealed contraband and that nearby Newcastle Cottage, on Trencrom Hill, was once a pub used by smugglers. So, too, was the *Old Albion*, at Crantock and the *Dolphin*, at Penzance. If Penzance could boast one smuggling pub, St. Ives could claim three or more, amongst them the *George and Dragon*, the *White Hart* and the *Blue Bell*.

Crackington Haven's once remote creek was greatly favoured by the illegal importers, while Tresillian creek was described, in 1701, as *'a most convenient place for the smuggling of foreign goods'*.

Not far from Tresillian – at King Harry Passage – an Exciseman on horseback riding in one direction, in August 1801, came face-to-face with a mounted smuggler going the other way. The latter turned and rode off at high speed down the road towards the river. Plunging into the Fal, he tried to get his horse to swim to the other side. However, before the beast had even reached the half-way mark, it showed every sign of exhaustion.

According to *The Royal Cornwall Gazette*: *'The intrepid rider slid from his back and, with his knife, cut the slings of the ankers and swam alongside his horse, exerting himself to keep his head above water, but all to no purpose; the horse was drowned, and the man with difficulty reached the shore. The less mettlesome Exciseman had halted on the shore, whence he surveyed the ineffectual struggle'.*

Fortunately for them, two Excise officers travelling from Luxulyan to Bodmin on a cold and bleak night four days before Christmas Eve 1805, fell amongst friends rather than enemies. Losing their way, they struck out blindly across the Goss Moor. Exhausted and near collapse, they were found by two tinners who heard their distressed groans and who *'going to their nightly labour, kindly relieved them, and thereby most probably saved their lives'*, *The Royal Cornwall Gazette* recorded.

A letter to *The West Briton*, published in April 1813, explains why the mayor of St. Mawes – a Customs officer – and two of his colleagues eventually paid substantial compensation to avoid standing trial for assault.

The letter tells that the mayor, a Mr. Jago, took it into his head that a worthy citizen, a Mr. Williamson, was involved in smuggling.

He and his colleagues had followed Mr. Williamson who, it seemed, was carrying a mysterious-looking box. *'One of his worship's men followed him, and seizing upon him with the grasp of a highwayman, he cried in the tone of one of that fraternity: "D—n you, deliver, what you have". This exclamation was followed by a struggle in which Mr. Williamson was forced to resign to the mayor of St. Mawes, a very valuable box of British jewellery. But the most extraordinary part of the business is that this box never reached the Custom-house; mind, Sir, I can't say how this has happened; his worship may have lost or mislaid it; I dare say it will be found yet . . . Yours etc. Jon. Thornberry,'*

If St. Mawes witnessed scenes of a rather informal and unofficial nature, then Fowey could match them when, in 1815, a French vessel put into the port and her cargo of spirits were taken to the Custom House. Again, *The West Briton* takes up the story: *'Here followed a most disgraceful scene; almost all concerned, including officers, extra-men, curiosity-men and pilfering-men, began to taste the welcome stuff. Such a division of the prey was productive of everything but harmony among the hunters, from words they came to blows . . . We cannot learn that the Magistrates interfered. The Recorder, we know, was a long way off! The Mayor is also non-resident without a deputy! The Deputy Recorder was perhaps too busily engaged in calculating his poundage as Collector! The senior Alderman (poor creature) is bed-ridden; The Senior Free-Burgess is Lord knows where, having paid his debt to nature near half a century since!'*

Fowey's Customs officers were not alone in taking – or allowing – liberties with impounded contraband. In 1827, the commander of the Revenue cutter *Lion* was in hot water for allowing his men to muscle-in on a successful recovery by crews from Polperro and Looe of tubs trawled up by the traditional method of 'creeping'. *Lion*'s men waded into the fray to grab their share of hte spirits with such enthusiasm that, in the frenzied attack on the tubs suspended from the sinking-rope, several of their Looe and Polperro colleagues had their fingers severely cut.

SAILING OUT ... An innocent fishing trip – or a journey to bring in brandy, silk and tobacco?

Chapter Seven

'I bribed the drivers not to interfere'

EXCITEMENT IN Falmouth could hardly be contained that day in April 1786. The Pellew brothers, working in conjunction with each other on the Revenue vessels *Hawk* and *Lark* had made a major capture of smugglers. The able-bodied and injured were both brought ashore and under strong escort taken to Pendennis Castle.

The men had been caught in the act. They had fired on Customs officers. They were in custody. They were on their way to eventual trial and severe penalties.

Or so it seemed.

But those who thought that the road from arrest to sentence was simple and automatic had overlooked one of the key weapons in the armoury of smuggling – audacity.

If threat and ingenuity failed, then audacity could sometimes win the day.

Few who understood the ways in which audacity could be deployed were surprised to read, a few days later, that although the smuggling vessel herself had been taken to Falmouth, the wounded lodged in secure sick quarters and the able-bodied behind thick walls and heavy doors at Pendennis Castle, that the story had not ended there.

A report from Falmouth, in the leading newspapers, gave a rather alarming account of how the arrests and detentions *'had caused a great stir in the town, the inhabitants being largely engaged in the smuggling trade. And as there was strong reason to fear a rescue – public sympathy being with the imprisoned smugglers – the authorities, having but an inadequate force at their disposal, appealed to government for assistance, and a company of soldiers was sent from Plymouth. In the meantime, communication having been established between the prisoners and their numerous sympathisers outside, 'ere the soldiers could arrive, the smugglers had forced their way out of the castle and, escorted by a numerous body of townsfolk, made their way into the country carrying with them all the wounded except one, who was too ill to be moved'.*

Audacity showed itself in a variety of ways – some expected, others totally out of character and, sometimes, seemingly motivated by nothing more than plain cheek rather than anticipated rewards.

In 1805, for instance, intruders raided the Customs store at Helford and removed a quantity of impounded roofing slates. If this had an air of unreality, then Dame Fortune restored the balance a year later when a Customs officer from Gweek was off-duty and out shooting. He wounded a bird in flight and, as he approached the point where it had dropped, he found sixty-three ankers of brandy.

The Royal Cornwall Gazette, of October 27, 1784, drew attention to the blatant way in which trading in smuggled goods had become an open operation in the county. A reader wrote: *'Lately passing through a neighbouring market town, I found **smuggled tobacco as publickly exposed for sale as any lawful commodity in the market.** Indeed, a person could scarcely pass a place where it was selling without having the article publickly recommended to him, with assurances of its goodness and cheapness and many importunities to buy. On making enquiry in the town concerning this traffic, I was credibly informed that many **hundreds weight** of smuggled traffic were sold there every market day. Surely such illicit traffic could be prevented in Cornwall were due attention paid to it by those whose duty it is to prevent a practice so disgraceful to the county, and so injurious to the fair trader'.*

In the early 1800s, one of the most famous of the Devon smugglers, John Rattenbury, of Beer, was captured. He was convicted at Falmouth where, obviously, a Cornish jury had no qualms about sending a Devonian to Bodmin gaol, and put in a carriage destined for the county prison.

Another smuggler shared the transport, together with two constables as an escort.

Rattenbury's audacity, not to mention his vanity, shows itself in his account of what happened next. *'When we came to Indian Queen, a public house a few miles from Bodmin, while the constables were taking their potations, I bribed the drivers not to interfere. Having finished, the constables ordered us into the chaise but we refused. A scuffle ensued. One of them collared me, some blows were exchanged, and he fired a pistol, the ball of which went off close to my head. My companion was engaged in encountering the other constable who called upon the drivers to assist, but they said it was their duty to attend the horses. We soon got the upper hand and, seeing a cottage near, I ran towards it and the woman who occupied it was so kind as to show me through the house and into the garden, and point out the road.*

'Toward evening we met a party of men who were smugglers like ourselves. They behaved handsomely and took us to a place called Newkey, where we slept. The next morning we got up very early and hired three horses for Mevagissey. We hired a boat which took us to Budleigh Salterton, that being the most convenient place to land as the wind was easterly. On the following day we walked on together and in the evening, to our great joy, arrived safe at Beer'.

A COSTLY LESSON ... Mitchell, where an excise officer made the mistake of trusting an informer. ▶

◀ *FISTICUFFS ... men came to blows in the St Ives pubs.*

In another escape on the road to Bodmin, several men were involved in an opportunist break for freedom. According to *The Royal Cornwall Gazette*, of October 3, 1807: *'whilst they were being loaded, one of the party, pretending a great deal of* **sang froid** *said to the turnkey: "Well, I have seen enough of this, so I'll be gone home". The turnkey, supposing him to be a mere spectator, who had been induced by curiosity to come in to see all the* **gieves** *put on the prisoners, opened the gate and the smuggler quietly walked off, rejoicing in the success of the scheme. Those who admire the ingenuity of the man will be sorry to learn that one of his own fraternity, with whom he had taken shelter, forfeited the rights of hospitality, and surrendered him again to the civil power'.*

Mr. Press, an Excise officer at Mitchell, learned a painful and expensive lesson at the hands of another cheeky smuggler.

He was contacted by a man calling himself Daw who offered, for a payment of £5, to show him where an illegal consignment of contraband was hidden near St. Austell. *'When they had walked some miles and got to an unfrequented part of the country, the fellow took the opportunity of tripping up the Officer's heels, when, seizing his pistols, he knelt on his breast and threatened to shoot him if he made any resistance, he robbed him of about £7 and his watch, with which, and the pistols, he made off, leaving the duped conservator of the revenue to make is way back as he could'*, *The West Briton* reported on 8th May 1818.

September 1840 saw the stage set for yet another impudent incident. Early in the month, a smuggling vessel approached the Cornish coast off Coverack. More than one hundred kegs of spirit were strung from bow to stern on either side. Seeing two men on the beach, the smugglers shouted to them to help drag the cargo ashore. They agreed but, when the landing was completed, the 'helpers' drew their pistols and declared themselves to be officers of the Coastguard. The smugglers fled, their vessel sailed and His Majesty's Customs and Excise were one large consignment of brandy to the good.

As the seizure occurred within the Gweek district, the brandy was taken to the warehouse at Helford for secure keeping.

Feeling that the entire episode reflected adversely on their own skill, as well as inconveniencing customers and delaying the payment of the proceeds, the smugglers decided to 'spring' what had been taken from them.

Early in the morning of September 18, between thirty and forty of them assembled outside the warehouse. Forcing the doors, they took all the kegs bar three and made off with their booty on several wagons they had brought with them. The operation took less than thirty minutes and thus suggested that a great deal of planning had gone into it.

Even more frustrating for the authorities was that the warehouse-keeper and his wife actually lived on the premises and were fully aware of the raid. They were unable to raise the alarm as, in their wisdom, H.M. Customs had sited the warehouse nearly three-quarters of a mile from the nearest dwelling.

And why were three kegs left?

Popular rumour had it that, having had the assistance of the Coastguard in landing the cargo, the smugglers felt that the least they could do was to invite their adversaries to have a drink on them!

The Sloop Inn, St. Ives, was a natural vantage-point for the many fights that took place between Excisemen and smugglers. Feelings ran so intensely between the two sides that any excuse to start a battle with fists, sticks and stones were eagerly seized. On Election Night 1820, a protest started with the burning of the effigy of a man who helped return two unpopular M.P.s to Westminster. Within an hour *'about 700 men, boys and women were all fighters together on the foresands, and great personal injury was inflicted.'* It was said that the red coat and cocked hat of an Exciseman had the same effect, in St. Ives, as waving a red rag at an angry bull.

Another act of audacity saved the day when a tailor from St. Just and a friend were on their way back to the town with a tub of brandy they had collected from the tunnel of a disused mine. To their horror, they saw an Exciseman approaching them. The tailor stood his ground but the companion dived into the bushes.

Not mincing his words, the Exciseman accused the tailor of smuggling. With the evidence so plainly visible, there was little point in denying it.

He explained, however, that he was a poor man with a sick wife and a large family.

The Exciseman had heard it all before.

The tailor then pretended to be cold, and asked if he could at least sample a drop or two for medicinal reasons.

His captor agreed.

The tailor's hands were so cold that he couldn't open the bung. Would the officer oblige, please?

As the official dismounted from horse and took the cask, the tailor jumped into the saddle and rode off. The Exciseman dropped the brandy and, as he ran off in pursuit of the fugitive, the friend re-emerged from the bushes, retrieved the spirit, and started to walk on to St. Just.

It was even said that some smugglers trained their horses to act like homing pigeons so that, if ordered to stop, the smuggler would throw himself from his mount, lashing the cask-laden horse to a gallop without the added burden of himself. Then, while he remained – free of incriminating visual evidence – to be questioned by the Exciseman, the horse would carry the load to a pre-arranged place of concealment.

Like many of the smuggling legends, it makes a good story!

KEIGWIN ARMS … The popular inn at Mousehole. ▶

▼ *ARMED ATTACK … The Customs House was rushed by an angry mob of smugglers.*

STORMY SEAS … Unbridled waves, fearsome gales and treacherous coastlines made putting to sea a hazardous business for smugglers and Revenue men alike.

Chapter Eight

'I wanted to run to call help from the Lord'

THE DIFFICULTY of being a Census officer is that, whatever might be locally known about the life and business of anyone included in the registrar, the entry has to be based on whatever information is actually volunteered by the person about to be listed.

The 1851 Census was no exception. Amongst the entries for Gunwalloe was: 'Henry Cuttance, victualler, born at St. Keverne'. There was no reference to his being one of the most gallant and quick-witted smugglers of his day, or to his official and unofficial trading as publican at the *Ship Inn*, Gunwalloe.

When seized by a Royal Navy party forcibly recruiting men, he was put on a warship on his way to impressed service. While the ship was three miles off-shore, he threw his hat overboard on one side and yelled: 'man overboard'. As the crew rushed excitedly to look, he jumped into the sea on the other side of the warship and swam safely back to the shore.

For most of his seventy-five years of life, Henry Cuttance, described as being a kind and courteous man, either took part in smuggling himself or else in the distribution and sale of contraband.

Yet his greatest and proudest claim to fame was not of the many times he outwitted his human enemies of the Preventive service, or the natural enemy of storm and sea, but the time he cheated death itself in what was to earn him a silver cup from the King of Norway, himself, and inscribed: *'Oscar, King of Norway, to Henry Cuttance of Gunwalloe, For brave and noble actions on the 20 Nov., 1846'*.

During a gale on that night, the Norwegian vessel *Elizabeth*, with a cargo of salt, was driven ashore at Gunwalloe. Within half-an-hour of hitting the rocks, *Elizabeth*, plus two crew members and the ship's boy were no more.

The captain and some other men were saved by Cuttance and a group of helpers. With no thought of their own safety, they scoured the rocks and the cliffs, braving waves and dashing into the seething surf to pluck seamen from the brink of death.

Even when they thought there were no more survivors, they continued their search and were rewarded when, in a cleft in a rock, they found another three men. These were so benumbed by cold and exposure that they could not help themselves and Cuttance and his colleagues dropped them a rope so that hot coffee and bread could be passed down. By-and-by a line with a chair slung to it, was lowered and the men were gradually lifted to safety after a rescue mission that had taken some ten hours to complete.

Their heroism was recognised by the Norwegian government who, in addition to King Oscar's presentation to Henry Cuttance, honoured the eight other rescuers with *'various pieces of plate as a reward'*. Additionally, the National Shipwreck Institution allocated *'the sum of five sovereigns to be distributed among the brave men, who, at the risk of their own lives, rescued the master and three crew of the late schooner brig* Elizabeth, *of Bergen, wrecked at Gunwalloe'*.

Although Henry Cuttance had five sons, Lisle, William, Eli, Warren and Joseph, it does not seem that they followed him into smuggling enterprises and that, unlike the Carters of Prussia Cove, there was no family business in which they all shared the risks and the profits.

The two main Carters were the brothers John and Harry. John, it seems, had the audacity and the daring, whereas Harry – a Methodist local preacher – kept his rather clouded light under a bushel in more senses than one.

GUNWALLOE ... Home of Henry Cuttance.

John Carter, who became well-known as the self-styled 'King of Prussia' escaped arrest on many occasions. To say that he courted captivity is an understatement. On one occasion, while he was away from Prussia Cove, the Customs broke into his lofts and took a large quantity of smuggled goods to the warehouse at Penzance.

Furious with the effrontery of the authorities, and worried that he could not deliver the contraband to his customers on the contracted date, Carter collected a force of volunteers, rode into Penzance, and reclaimed their goods. When the Excisemen arrived at the shattered door of the store next morning, it was as obvious who had perpetrated the recovery as if John Carter's fingerprints had been left behind as the only goods taken were those that had, in their turn, been seized at Prussia Cove. As the report on the incident put it: *'John Carter has been here, and we know it because he is an upright man, and has taken away nothing that was not his own'*.

John decided to fortify the cove against possible attack from Revenue cutters and built a fortification that would have done credit to a more formally-designed castle!

The defences were put to the test in 1803 when sabre-rattling between John Carter and the Customs reached a show-down. Two years earlier one of his vessels intercepted the Revenue cutter *Brilliant* as she made for Penzance loaded with recovered contraband. Carter's men boarded her, captured her, evacuated her crew, emptied her of all the seized cargo, then set her adrift – all within sight of Newlyn harbour.

On that day, in 1803, one of the King of Prussia's craft cut it rather fine and, under hot pursuit from the Revenue cutter *Faery*, made for the safety of the guns of the battery.

Using their intimate knowledge of the rocks and reefs, Carter's men ran through a narrow channel in the rocks to safety. *Faery* dropped anchor and sent a boat in, only to be bombarded by Carter's guns. The boat's crew retreated and, for several hours, *Faery* and the 'garrison' fired ineffectually at

▲ *PRUSSIA COVE … Lofts were searched in the hunt for smuggled goods.*

▼ *DEFENCES … John Carter fortified Prussia Cove to keep control of his 'kingdom'.*

one another while reinforcements rushed by road from Penzance.

They too were unable to get through the hail of fire from the 'castle' and, after a few more hours of total stalemate, the cutter resumed her patrol; the troops returned to Penzance; and Carter and his men lived to smuggle another day.

John Carter himself seems to have disappeared from the smuggling scene by 1807, possibly due to the cooling of the international temperature between Britain and France. Indeed, the story is told of the sailor who came back to Marazion from the Napoleonic wars. His parents asked him for news and he told them: *'The King of Prussia's 'ad a gert loss'.* His parents shook their head in dismay: *'My dear life, 's that really so? I tell 'ee I'm really sorry for that dear man. Wasn't it only last month as someone told on'n an' he lost nigh on forty kegs of brandy'.*

Harry Carter was a more interesting member of the family as, almost as if to clear himself of any connection with smuggling, he wrote an interesting book on his life and travels in which he only occasionally gave clues as to his illegal activities – possibly because most of his colleagues were still alive and could be easily identified and prosecuted.

In 1778, he was arrested in France but was exchanged for a French captive taken by the Royal Navy. The French, however, had confiscated his own vessel and imprisoned the thirty-five man crew.

Obviously reluctant to learn the lesson, or assuming that lightning in the form of arrest could not strike twice, Carter went back to Cornwall.

'So, after I was at home some time, riding about the country getting freights, collecting money for the company, etc., we bought a cutter with nineteen guns. I went in her some time smuggling. I had great success'.

HIS KINGDOM … John Carter's realm.

ON THE SHORE … Crates and casks must be safely stowed but some can take their ease.

The Carter 'company' consisted in the main of Harry looking after the buying and transportation of goods and John dealing with the landing and the distribution.

It was Harry, however, who took the risks. He certainly played a double game and, on some occasions, was used by the Royal Navy as an auxiliary to pursue and capture French vessels in Cornish waters. In one incident, in which his own vessel was badly damaged by gunfire, he rescued seventeen of the thirty-one crew of a French cutter with which he had been fighting.

He tells of a frightening experience when his own lugger was boarded, off Cawsand by the Royal Navy: *'My people having some muskets, dropt them down and went below. I knowing nothing of that, thought all would stand by me. I begun to encourage them as well as I could without anything in my hands, as they took us in surprise so suddenly, I having my great coat buttoned about me, I seeing none of my people, only one man at the helm; and when they saw no person to oppose them, turned upon me with their broad swords, and begun to beat away upon my head. I found the blows very heavy – crushed me down to the deck – and as I never loosed my senses, rambled forward. They still pursued me, beating and pushing me, so that I fell down on the deck on a small raft just out of their way'.*

He thought it best to pretend to be dead and carried out the pretence for several hours. Eventually an officer *'put his hand up under my clothes, between my shirt and my skin, and then examined my head, and so concluded, saying: "The man is so warm now as he was two hours back, but his head is all to atoms". I have thought hundreds of times since what a miracle it was that I neither sneezed, coughed, nor drew breath that they perceived in all this time, I suppose not less than ten or fifteen minutes'.*

Carter waited until darkness and decided to try to get ashore.

'As I was lifting myself over the side, I was taken with the cramp in one of my thighs. So then I thought I should be drowned, but still willing to risk it, so that I let myself over the side very easily by a rope fearing my enemies would hear me. As I was very near the shore, I thought to swim onshore in the course of a stroke or two as I used to swim so well, but soon found out my mistake. I was sinking almost like a stone, and hauling astern in deeper water, when I gave up all hopes of life, and begun to swallow some water'.

Miraculously, he survived but found: *'The bone of my nose cut right in two, nothing but a bit of skin holding it, and two very large cuts in my head, that two or three bits of skull worked out afterwards; and after so long laying on the deck with that very cold weather, and being not alltogether drowned, but allmoste, I think I did not know I was wounded or loste any blood'.*

The experience increased the strong religious awareness that Harry Carter had always possessed and he became a preacher with fire, conviction and rigid rules. He would not tolerate swearing or profanity on board his ships: *'I allwayse had a dislike to swearing, and made a law on board, if any of the sailors should swear, was poneshed. Nevertheless my intention was not pure; I had sume byends in it, the bottom of it was only pride, etc. I wanted to be noted to be sumething out of the common way of others, still I allwayse had a dislike to hear others swearing.'*

He preached in Cornwall, in New York, in Guernsey and in Roscoff where he would insist that all British smugglers in the port on a Sunday morning should come to his impromptu quay-side services. He wrote: *'The men took off their hats, all very serious, no laffing and no trifling conversations'.*

Yet Captain Harry Carter, man of great personal courage and daring, doubted his own ability to preach of his own faith and experience and to fire others with religious conviction. As that perverse and canvassed congregation gathered on the quay-side at Roscoff: *'I begun to tremble and sweat, I could scarcely hold the hymn book in both hands . . . I had not the least thoughts to say anything and I wanted to run to call for help from the Lord . . . so that when I roase from my knees I was surprised to see so many hard hearts to their knees so that I found much curage to go on in my poor simple way'.*

Chapter Nine

'The chase is not to be given up'

ALTHOUGH there was some truth in the popular statement that a Cornish jury would never convict a Cornish smuggler, the real explanation of why there were seemingly so few arrests and, accordingly, so few convictions, lay in the law itself rather than in the sentimentality of jurors.

Judges were obliged to remind juries that conviction depended upon there being absolute certainty that the spirit and the procedures of the law had been wholly followed.

Often it seemed the very rules of H.M. Customs and Excise made it impossible to make a 'legal' arrest.

In 1832, officers were told: *'When a vessel is chased, and the goods are thrown overboard, the chase is not to be given up to take possession of such goods, but the pursuit is to be continued whilst there is any possibility of coming up with, and securing, the vessel and crew; and in order that all chance of recovering the goods may not be lost, a "Mark Buoy" is to be thrown overboard at such time as may appear most likely to lead to their discovery; observing that if the goods are floating, a buoy should be thrown amongst them, with a view to it drifting with them, and affording, in the event of their being found, a proof of their identity'.*

The thought behind the instruction was good and clear – catch the smuggler at all costs; don't chase abandoned goods; but recover anything thrown overboard once the smugglers have been caught.

However, the reality was a little daunting. If the Customs cutter did not collect the abandoned goods, there might be no evidence against the smugglers. If the cutter continued the chase, it did not follow that the vessel it was chasing would be overtaken. And if the floating casks and bundles were clearly marked, there was every chance that by the time the cutter returned, another smuggling-craft would have collected them and spirited away.

Thus a Customs officer who followed the rules could lose captives and contraband. However, one who disregarded the rules could see the case thrown out of court on a technicality.

Even worse was the following instruction: *'When a vessel is seized or detained on suspicion, at sea, the Officer in Command of the Cruizer or boat making the seizure is to take particular care that the soundings are immediately taken, and that the distance from the shore at the precise time be clearly ascertained by causing two points of land, or remarkable fixed objects on the shore to be set, and the bearings thereof to be noted by two or more Officers, or persons well acquainted therewith, so that each of them may be able to swear to the bearings to the course that the vessel was steering when first seen, and to her subsequent proceedings . . .'*

Once more, these were seemingly simple requirements with which to secure an arrest; recover contraband; and satisfy magistrates that an offence of illegal importation had been committed within British Territorial Waters.

An instruction was one thing. But a clever defence before a Court or jury, often in total ignorance of the relevance of navigational bearings, could demolish the entire evidence as having been illegally engineered by H.M. Customs and Excise.

Positive identification of jettisoned goods was vital. But since barrels and bales rarely carried distinguishing marks, it could always be argued by the defence that they had either been 'planted' or had been seized by Revenue officers on another occasion and merely been recycled in the hope of a further conviction.

Similarly, the requirement to prove a precise navigational 'fix' was always open to challenge, since those in the dock could have it claimed for them that, in the excitement of hot pursuit, the comman-

THE CHASE … is not to be given up.

der of the Revenue craft might not have had the necessary manpower free to be able to provide the called-for *'two or more Officers, or persons well-acquainted thereof'* to have taken the required bearings and soundings *'immediately'* as was rigidly demanded by the instruction.

Indeed, if the Crown's case sought to bring in the serious allegations that the smugglers had opened fire, then the existence of flying shot and other missiles would make it even more unlikely that, in the heat of the fray, a couple of officers were calmly standing on the deck of the Revenue cruiser and taking bearings.

A series of Acts of Parliament made smuggling legislation more like black comedy than something that could be taken totally seriously.

An act of 1721 *'to prevent the clandestine running of Goods and the Danger of Infection thereby'* laid down that brandy could only legally be imported by large vessels calling at major ports, thus ruling any such cargo carried by a small boat automatically illegal. The same Act directed the principal officers of His Majesty's Customs to seize such boats and *'to cause the Hull of such Ship, Vessel or Boat to be burnt and wholly destroyed, and the Tackle, Furniture and Apparel thereunto belonging, to be publickly sold to the best Advantage.'* Any convicted smuggler *'shall be judged guilty of Felony, and shall, for such his, her or their Offence, be transported as a Felon to some or one of His Majesty's Colonies or Plantations in America, there to remain for the Space of Seven Years.'*

If any such convicted and transported person escaped from the plantations and returned to Britain, they *'shall suffer as Felons, and have Execution awarded against him, her or them as Persons attainted of*

Felony, without Benefit of Clergy'.

Any accomplices informing upon members of the team would receive immunity from arrest and trial *'and receive the Sum of Forty Pounds for every such Offender so discovered and convicted, as a Reward for such his Discovery'*. They could also expect a 'recognition' in the form of a percentage of the value of any illegal goods taken into custody as a consequence of their information.

A later Act, in 1735, increased the informer's reward to £50 a head in respect of two or more persons being arrested, provided those arrested were armed. Anyone who had over 6lbs of tea on which duty had not been paid was liable to be declared a smuggler.

It was even an offence to loiter within five miles of the coast without good reason. Conviction, since it was assumed that a loiterer could be a look-out, included flogging as an alternative to imprisonment. Eventually hanging was introduced when transportation seemed to lack any effective purpose as a deterrent.

Ten years later – in 1745 – came another Act. This one recognised that successful smuggling involved a community turning a blind eye. Accordingly, if smugglers stole back an impounded cargo from a Customs warehouse, the community could be fined £200. If a Customs officer was assaulted, the community had to pay £20. If one was killed, the penalty was £100. However, if someone was convicted within six months of the commission of the offence, the community penalty was repaid.

If a suspected smuggler was arrested more than thirty days after he had committed a crime, the Customs officer making the arrest received a bounty of £500.

The automatic effect of this was to ensure that no incident resulted, other than unavoidably, in anyone being arrested inside the first month following an assault or a murder!

The only good thing that came out of the Act of 1745 was that smugglers who wished to renounce their old ways were given an amnesty and a free pardon provided they joined the Royal Navy and

WAYSIDE GRAVE … Executed smugglers were given cursory burial at the roadside.

stayed in the Service until discharged on grounds of age or disability.

The 1745 Act kept alive one of the more bizarre sections of an earlier one, whereby: *'Persons who shall be found passing (knowingly and willingly) with any Foreign Goods or Commodities landed from any Ship or Vessel, without the due Entry and Payment of the Duties, in their Custody, from any of the Coasts of this Kingdom, or within twenty miles of any of the said Coasts; and shall be more than five persons in company, or shall carry any offensive Arms or Weapons, or wear any Vizard, Mask or other Disguise when passing with such Goods, or shall forcibly hinder or resist any officer of the Customs and Excise in the selling of Run-Goods, shall be Guilty of Felony and be transported for seven years to some or other of His Majesty's Plantations or Colonies in America'.*

Any person convicted of smuggling silk or cloth must be sentenced, the Magistrates' Manual for 1772 advised: *'to be whipped and set in the stocks; to be then committed to prison or house of correction till satisfaction be made or punishment inflicted'.*

Parliament was told: *'In some parts of the maritime counties the whole people are so generally engaged in smuggling that it is impossible to find a jury that will, on trial, do justice to an officer of the Revenue in any case whatever. In these counties where smuggling has become so general, the majority of the coroners' inquests juries always consist of smugglers, so that it has been found by experience that these inquests always bring the officer and his assistants in guilty of murder, even though it be made clearly to appear by the most undoubted testimonies that the killing happened* de defendo'.

HOME OF THE ASSIZES … Launceston, with its castle and much-feared gaol, was a name to strike dread into the hearts of the smugglers.

ARCHWAY ... The way to the cells at Launceston.

Having tackled the smugglers and their associates, the law then turned to seeking to control the type of vessels actually used. In 1816, a regulation demanded the forfeiture of any cutter, lugger, wherry, sloop, smack or yawl having a bowsprit which extended in length to more than two thirds the length of the hull. This effectively removed fast boats from the resources of smugglers. The regulation was strengthened by then demanding the forfeiture of the Cornish smugglers' favourite craft, luggers of over fifty tons.

New edicts from Whitehall set out the method of construction; materials; proportions; measurements; plant thicknesses and even the position of timbers. The size of the permitted crew was related to the tonnage of the vessel and any surplus of manpower was regarded as an automatic admission of illegal activities.

In future, all boats, carriages, carts and waggons discovered in smuggling use would be forfeit to the Crown and be broken up. Horses would be seized.

Any person who, while engaged in smuggling, *'shall have his face blacked, or shall wear any mask or other disguise, shall be adjudged guilty of felony and shall suffer death'*. However, unlike the convicted smuggler, the accomplice would be allowed 'the benefit of clergy' on his last trip to the gallows.

Such repressive laws led to a catalogue of unsatisfactory verdicts and sentences in cases that came before the courts in Cornwall.

Although John Leane, of Gwennap, helped Customs officers recover ten ankers of gin of the twenty-two 'liberated' from the Custom House at Truro, in March 1801, he was still charged with the theft of the balance and received the obligatory sentence of seven years' transportation.

Richard Cock was tried by a special jury at Cornwall Assizes, in April 1815, charged with lighting a fire on the cliffs at Rame Head to warn smugglers that Revenue officers were in the vicinity. He denied the offence but, being unable to prove that the two separate blazes he had been seen igniting were for any other purpose, he was convicted and sent to America.

A letter to *The West Briton*, on December 12, 1817, told of the heavy-handedness accorded another prisoner, John Hughes, who was remanded to Bodmin gaol because he could not raise adequate bail.

He was held 'for nearly four months, confined with the felons, during which time he was heavily ironed, and underwent the same treatment that is most usually extended to the most criminal of his class. He was sent from Bodmin, ironed as the felons, to take his trial at Launceston and, when there, was dismissed on account of no-one appearing before him.

'Shortly after his return to his family, he was summoned to appear before the magistrates at Truro; he did so, and a second time no-one appeared against him. Saturday was the third time that this poor fellow was torn apart from his family by these lenient officers, to appear on this business.

'It was certainly gratifying to hear what was said by two professional Gentlemen, who pointed out the extreme hardship and illegality of the proceedings of the Officers and consequently paid no compliment to their wisdom or mercy'.

John Pitts, a Mevagissey fisherman, was only striking a light for his pipe when he was arrested by a Preventive officer just before Christmas 1824 – or that was his story!

The jury decided to believe the prosecution after hearing that as the officer was rowing ashore after a fruitless search of Pitts' boat, he spotted a light being signalled from the shore. Looking back towards the boat he had just left, he saw Pitts making a light. *'I took the defendant and his companion into custody'*, the officer testified.

At the Cornwall Summer Assize of 1835, a group of smugglers was charged with assaulting Coastguards, and *with assisting others in landing and carrying away prohibited goods, some being armed with offensive weapons'.*

The charges arose from an incident in which an officer, named Harper, had chased the men after they had collected a cargo of contraband from the beach at Lantic, near Fowey. Ignoring the fact that he and his five colleagues were outnumbered, they called on the smugglers to surrender although every one of them was carrying either a stick or a club.

Warning them that *'if you touch a man or a tub, you will all be murdered'*, the smugglers tried to get away. The officers closed in and, after a violent struggle in which one officer was beaten unconscious, five were taken prisoner.

The defence tried to get Harper to admit that the sticks were not different to the walking sticks usually carried by men in the country. The Crown pointed out how dangerous they were and how viciously they had been used. Even the judge enlarged on this by saying that the villains were lucky not to be facing a murder charge as it was purely by good fortune that one of the Coastguards had not been killed in the melee.

Yet despite the evidence, the jury returned a verdict of 'not guilty', adding their opinion that the sticks were not offensive weapons.

Even more unbelievable was the fact that although the five accused men were all known to have a dubious and violent reputation, a local clergyman and a dozen farmers from Lanreath and St. Germans appeared as character witnesses.

There was little doubt however, that Revenue officers – and their service – were heartily disliked by the law-abiding community every bit as much as by the smugglers. An item in *The West Briton*, of March 3, 1826, carried the following report: *'On Sunday se'nnight, just as the church bells at St. Columb had announced the time of morning service, a post-chaise driving rapidly into the town attracted the attention*

DESERTED VILLAGE … Port Quin – did villagers flee from fear?

of the town's people, then proceeding to church. The chaise stopped at the inn and forth came a supervisor and another officer of Excise, and commenced, forthwith, a general search, as was supposed, for smuggled spirits etcetera. After they had satisfied themselves that they had been put on a wrong scent, or that the objects of their search had been put beyond their reach, they proceeded to the village of Mawgan, in the neighbourhood, without any better success.

'On their return at night, after taking necessary refreshment, they were about to enter the chaise in order to leave – or rather one of them had got in – when their olfactory nerves were saluted with a powerful odour from something with which the seat had been covered during their absence. A speedy retreat was made from the polluted vehicle, but which, after it had undergone a cleansing process, they were compelled to enter, however uninviting the exhalations that saluted them; and in which they drove off amidst the cheers of the spectators'.

Certainly the authoritarian and often violent behaviour of some Excise officers earned the loathing of the public in many parts of Cornwall.

In 1804, for instance, the credibility of the Service took a severe knock when, undoubtedly, an officer used excessive and unwarranted force against a man who was so obviously guilty of smuggling that he would, no doubt have given himself up after token resistance. *The Royal Cornwall Gazette*, of December 8, 1804, reported: *'John Stephens was committed to the County prison at Bodmin a few days ago, charged with the wilful murder of Richard Pentecost, in the parish of St. Keverne. It appears that Stephens, who belongs to the new office of Inspection, met with Pentecost and another man with smuggled goods in their possession, which he attempted to seize; and hence arose the scuffle which ended so fatally'.*

But if the people of St. Columb scored a notable success in using something rather unpleasant to drive unwanted Revenue officers away, the question will always arise as to whether or not the Revenue men caused the evacuation and total abandonment of a quaint fishing village near Wadebridge.

Port Quin was, until the dawn of the 1800s, a pretty and isolated village where men made their living from the sea. In most weathers they fished. In all weathers they dabbled in smuggling and the distribution of smuggled goods. Then, in the course of one dramatic night, the entire population disappeared. They left food in the cupboards, dishes on the tables, clothes in their rooms. Everything, in fact, that adds up to the signs of a classic emergency evacuation.

Today, almost two hundred years later, the cottages still stand alongside the road, their roofs collapsed; their walls still identifiable through thick ivy. Yet there is still no evidence as to why a community should have disappeared so dramatically and suddenly.

Among a dozen possible theories, three seem to tie in with the conditions of the Cornwall of those days.

Firstly, that a ship was in distress off the harbour and that the men of the village were all lost as they rowed to the rescue, leaving a man-less community from which the widows and the womenfolk moved.

Then there's the disease possibility. It could be that Port Quin was devastated by one of the many cholera epidemics that raged through Cornwall and that, having buried their dead, the survivors melted into the surrounding countryside to try to forget the horror they had experienced.

Finally, there is the Customs legend. This is that, hearing from an informer of an imminent raid on the village by Customs and Dragoons, the people of Port Quin abandoned their homes and their possessions and took safety in flight.

◄ SMUGGLERS' TRANS-
PORT ... *Carts and wagons were seized.*

PROCESS OF LAW ... ►
Bodmin, where an excise officer was charged with murder.

SMUGGLERS' HAVEN …
Rock, by the Camel – one of the
North Cornish sites well-known
for its smuggling activities
throughout the 18th century.

Chapter Ten

'So callous in her conscience and deadly in her revenge'

EVEN HAD they not been involved in smuggling, they could have been described – with no pun intended – as a 'rum collection' of ill-assorted personalities with such names as Black Joan, The Fyns, Doga, Old Worm and Cruel Coppinger.

They were, individually, amongst the most cunning, violent and treacherous people who spanned some two hundred years of Cornish smuggling and left behind them reputations that firmly laid to rest any would-be fiction that smugglers were really rather decent people only looking for excitement in their various illegal activities.

Coppinger stepped out of the worst tradition of the Vikings. He was a Dane who arrived in Cornwall amidst all the majesty and aura of a horrendous hurricane. Folk-lore had it that, thrown on the shore by the force of the storm, he ripped a shawl from the back of an old woman who had gone to the beach to witness the shipwreck, and was immediately befriended by another sightseer – a farmer's daughter – who took him to the farm where he was clothed, fed and made welcome in every conceivable way!

He convinced the farmer that he was of noble birth and duly married the daughter. Sadly, their only child was deaf and dumb and mentally retarded. Even worse, its only pleasure was to copy its father's rather unpleasant habit of torturing all living things. Rumour even had it that Coppinger's child murdered one of its playmates.

Unhappy about the design of boats available on the North Cornish coast, Coppinger went back to Denmark and returned with his own schooner, *Black Prince,* with which he began his smuggling operations.

He never experienced difficulties in getting a crew. Anyone who crossed him had a simple choice – either serve on board *Black Prince* or risk torture, mutilation or death. He often wounded or maimed for no better reason or necessity than that it underlined his ruthlessness and reduced the courage of those who might oppose him.

Coppinger, it was claimed, had as colourful a passing as had been his introduction to Cornwall and his career as a smuggler.

'At length', it is recorded, *'the time came for the fiend to claim his own. Several persons and other pious folk were sent for and readily came, for the dying sinner was rich. Although it was harvest-time and high-by-day, the old wrecker's chamber became, at times, as dark as night. The parsons saw the devil in the room when others could not; and by their reading they drove him to take many shapes, but for all that he would not be put out, and at last, when the devil took the form of a fly and buzzed about the dying wretch, they saw it was in vain for them to try any longer. During all the time the exorcists were thus engaged, the death chamber seemed – by the sound – to be filled with the sea splashing around the bed, and the waves were heard as if surging and breaking against the house, "though it was a good bit inland".*

If the story is to be believed, Coppinger's burial was every bit as spectacular as his death. As the coffin was taken towards the church, there was a sudden storm *'and a tempest blew up with such violence that the bearers could scarcely keep on their legs to reach the churchyard stile, where such sheets of blinding lightning flashed around them that they dropped the coffin and rushed into the church'.*

Almost as socially unpleasant as Cruel Coppinger were the Fyns, a brother and sister team of smugglers who used Looe Island as their base. Miss Fyn – Black Joan – to her friends and foes alike, was rather unladylike both in her flow of language and her use of her fists to such devastating effect that

CONTRACT CONTRABAND … A smuggling farmer had a regular contract to supply this inn at Pool.

she punched many men senseless. She rowed a boat, smoked and always dressed like a man. The favourite menu of this weird couple consisted of any wild rats they could catch on the island.

They introduced a very effective signalling service with which to warn smugglers of the whereabouts of Revenue officers. A colleague would ride his white horse along the mainland coast facing the island. If he remained in the saddle, then all was well. If he dismounted and returned on foot, this meant trouble. Either way, one of the Fyns would then pass a pre-arranged signal, by lights or flags, to the smuggling craft waiting out at sea.

Richard Pentreath, of Mousehole, was known as 'Doga'. Writing of him, in 1771, the Penzance Collector of Customs described him as *'an honest man in all his doings though a notorious smuggler'*. The Collector also seemed to respect another Mousehole man, Thomas Mann, recorded as *'a reputed smuggler, but an honest man'*.

Veryan boasted a multi-talented law-breaking son.

Robert Long dabbled in piracy and theft as well as in smuggling. However, in 1661 he was arrested, tried and sentenced to death by hanging. As an example to others, he was hanged in chains at the crossroads between Ruan Lanihorne and St. Mawes. Some time later, his decomposing body was taken down and interred in a roadside grave.

John Knill, of St. Ives, led a double life. His respectability lay in that he was a Collector of Customs from 1762-82 as well as being Mayor in 1767.

The disreputable side of Knill was that, throughout most of the period that he was pursuing and prosecuting smugglers, he was a smuggler himself. On one occasion a ship ran aground near Hayle. When officers went on board the abandoned vessel, they found it packed with goods seemingly intend-

SENNEN … Where contraband was linked with conflict.

JOHN KNILL'S STEEPLE …
Built by the Mayor of St Ives who was Collector of Customs from 1762 to 1782 – and who was thought to have lived the double life of a smuggler as well.

THE SENNEN INN … reputed to be the 'resort of all the idle blackguards in the county.'

ed for illegal importation. On the instruction of John Knill, the ship's papers were destroyed. It was believed that these would have identified Knill and Squire Praed, of Trevetho, as being the shippers of the contraband.

Along the coast, above Portreath, was William Burgess's farm, Trengrove. Burgess, who lived from 1766 to 1862, was a farmer as well as a smuggler. Not only did he smuggle, distribute and sell, but he had regular contracts with *Tyack's Hotel*, in Camborne, and the *Plume of Feathers*, at Pool.

Talland Church, near Looe, had a memorial to Robert Mark, late of Polperro, who was shot dead by Customs officers in January 1802.

> 'In prime of life most suddenly
> Sad tidings to relate
> Here view my utter destiny
> And pity my sad fate
> I, by a shot that rapid flew
> Was instantly struck dead.
> Lord pardon the offender who
> My precious blood did shed
> Grant him to rest and forgive
> All I have done amiss
> And that I may rewarded be
> With everlasting bliss.'

Looe Island had its brother and sister, the Fyns. Madron had the Pollard brothers, Christopher and Joseph.

Christopher had long been known as a smuggler but, when an amnesty was granted in 1803, he per-

HELL'S MOUTH ... The formidable cliffs were a deterrent to discovery when goods were being landed on the beach below.

suaded Joseph to put up the necessary £200 surety so that he could make amends.

His period of honesty did not last long. By 1805 he was already in hot water, having been charged with assaulting Excise officers at Sennen; attempting to recover contraband that had been lawfully seized; and inciting a crowd of between three and four hundred persons to attack the officers.

Pollard's version was rather different. Far from having used the violent and improper language alleged by the prosecution, he had been a mere bystander. Not only had he not incited anyone to do anything improper, but he had walked quietly home, pausing only to call at the Excise office in Newlyn to warn the officers there that they ought to go immediately to Sennen as it appeared that trouble was brewing.

A companion said that, at Sennen, they found a huge crowd firing muskets and throwing stones at the beleagured officials. *'We decided that was no place for us to stay as we might be killed, so we both returned home'*.

The Crown's case depended on its star witness, one Anne George. She, with her husband, Joseph, had run the *Sennen Inn* for several years until their reputation and behaviour made them too unsavoury for even that job. The inn, which was a market-place for smuggled goods and a meeting-place for those involved in organising ventures, was described as *'the resort of all the idle blackguards in the county'* and thus had arguably the worst name of any hostelry in Cornwall.

Joseph George, while landlord, acted as go-between for the actual owner of the pub, Dionysius Williams. Believing that he had enough evidence with which to keep Williams in a permanent fear of blackmail, Joseph decided to stop paying rent. After the arrears had reached an unacceptable level, Dionysius threw the Georges out, saying he would call their bluff.

It turned out to be very unwise as, within weeks, Dionysius Williams was starting a very long sentence having been convicted on the testimony of Anne George after she had turned King's evidence against him and thus escaping the prosecution of her husband and herself.

If this painted a rather unpleasant picture of Anne George, it was only the tip of a very nasty iceberg.

In 1802 she had a row with Joseph's brother, John, over a few pounds of tobacco. Once more she turned King's evidence to get her own back. On June 5, 1802, he was hanged on her venomous testimony.

Now to get Christopher Pollard into prison, she was to be used again by the prosecution. The defence had been warned of her treachery, and counsel's brief noted: *'The terror and dismay, indeed, which this woman has been the means of spreading throughout the county are not to be described. Independent of the present prosecution no less than five persons have been capitally indicted by her means, one of whom has already been executed, and so callous is her conscience, and deadly her revenge, that persons who may have given her slight cause for offence are now trembling for fear of the consequences, expecting to be made the next victim of the detestable passion with which she is actuated'.*

For once she was totally discredited and, as a result, Pollard was acquitted of all the charges against him. Unfortunately he did not, even then, appreciate the inevitability of arrest and conviction if he continued smuggling.

Ten years later he was committed to prison after being arrested off Plymouth with a large quantity of contraband.

Like Falmouth, Penzance and St. Ives, Fowey was served by a smuggling Mayor. In 1824 he was invited to the Custom House to assist in inquiries into the arrival of a large quantity of brandy hidden on a French cutter. He declined to assist and, initially, refused officers permission to search his home. He gave way then they returned with a warrant.

While officers were listing wine and brandy left surprisingly openly in a ground-floor room, they heard sounds of frantic action upstairs. As they broke down the door of a bedroom they found the Mayor feverishly smashing bottles so that evidence would soak away. Just how successful he had been could not be assessed, but other contraband worth some £300 was seized and later resulted in a very successful prosecution.

Captain James Williams, the noted St. Ives smuggler, rejoiced in the strange nickname 'Old Worm'. He smuggled blatantly using his fishing smack, *St. George*. He had a charmed life and always seemed to be at least two jumps ahead of the authorities. This often had the result that, in their frustration, they used various irregularities to try to catch him red-handed.

Indignant after his boat had been detained merely because a piece of sacking casually thrown over the stern had obscured three letters of her name, 'Old Worm' wrote a long, articulate and blistering letter to the local newspapers protesting about the breach of procedure, and suggesting that the officer concerned had been too drunk to know what he was doing.

He wrote: *'The general belief in this town and neighbourhood is, that as one of the Coastguard, named Cock, was rambling from a public house late on Saturday night, he fancied he met a waggon loaded with contraband goods, and in his attempt to stop the waggon was either knocked down, or for some other cause fell under the waggon. This circumstance has led to the detention of my vessel, as at that time she was the only one in the bay . . . how far they have a right to detain the ship I am at a loss to conceive. Had this occurred in any other port I should with my crew be in a state of very great distress. I am a native of this port and am in consequence thrown upon my friends for my daily bread'.*

The letter worked and the detention of *St. George* was lifted. However, the Customs were not to be thwarted and, four days later – perhaps too conveniently – a length of rope attached to some casks of spirits crept up was found to correspond with that used on board Captain William's boat. He was arrested, charged with smuggling, and sent for trial.

There were no witnesses and he was freed, the trial – in 1851 – bringing a virtual end to smuggling prosecutions in Cornwall's courts.

Customs officers in Kent thought they had an open and shut case when they detained the vessel *Admiral Hood* following a chase in which the crew of the Revenue cruiser *Lively* had clearly seen tubs being thrown overboard. After *Admiral Hood* had been boarded, the tubs were recovered from the sea and were found to contain spirits.

Nothing could have been simpler than to obtain a quick conviction, they reckoned.

But they were wrong. A certain Sir William Courtenay appeared before the magistrates and swore that although he had witnessed the entire incident, no tubs had been thrown from *Admiral Hood* and that those on board *Lively* had, in his sight, been recovered long before the smuggling vessel came on the scene.

It looked as if the prosecution case would collapse in the light of such a statement from so substantial a figure as Sir William Courtenay, Knight of Malta.

Investigations took place and it was soon established that, on the day and at the time of the incident, Sir William was actually twenty-five miles from the scene and sitting in his regular pew in church. He was promptly charged with perjury and put up for trial at Maidstone Assizes in July 1833.

ATLANTIC WAVES … Porthmeor Beach, St Ives with the ocean in a gentle mood.

BLACKMAIL AND TREACHERY … The tranquil Sennen cottages concealed dreadful secrets.

Many shocks were in store. Far from being Sir William Courtenay, K.M., it was discovered that he was John Nichols Thom, who had been born at St. Columb Major on November 10, 1799 to 'Cracked Charity' as his mother was known. She was to die in the county lunatic asylum.

To say that he was a weird boy is an understatement. While at school he was expelled for cutting the whiskers off the headmistress' favourite cat. He was involved in several incidents in which offices, houses and building with which he was connected fell victim to mysterious fires. Those who knew him agreed that 'there's a screw loose somewhere'.

In 1832 he finally cracked and set off on a holy pilgrimage, proclaiming himself to be Sir William Courtenay, Knight of Malta and *'forerunner of the expected Messiah'*, having' *travelled from the County of Cornwall to announce to the people of the East the approaching advent of the Messiah'*.

Denounced as a religious maniac, he returned to England from his travels with the even more majestic title of 'Sir William Percy Honeywood Courtenay, Knight of Malta, King of Jerusalem and Prince of Abysinnia' and, as such, sought election as Member of Parliament for Canterbury in December 1832.

He attracted three hundred and seventy-five of the nineteen hundred votes cast. Encouraged by his 'success' he travelled the towns and villages of Kent campaigning, amongst other things, against the revenue laws. It was in this context that he openly befriended smugglers.

The Kent jury took little time to convict him and he was sentenced to three months for perjury and seven years transportation for supporting smuggling. For some strange reason, friends made representations to the Home Secretary that the sentence of the court should not be carried out and that he should be registered as insane.

REGISTERED INSANE … John Nichols Thom, the child born to 'Cracked Charity' was to attract followers and incite bloodshed before being himself killed in a fearsome battle.

The Home Secretary agreed and, for five years, Thom was a patient at the Barming Heath lunatic asylum. Despite his detention, he still wanted to be elected to Parliament and issued a string of addresses to his followers and managed to influence local elections to a considerable extent.

In 1838, giving way to political pressure, Lord John Russell unwisely used his powers as Home Secretary to order the release of Thom from the asylum. Immediately, the madman resumed his crusades and tramped the highways and byways of Kent holding forth.

On May 31, 1838, Thom and fifteen supporters 'preached' to an audience that was so enthusiastic that several farm labourers deserted the fields to join his followers. The furious farmer went to a local magistrate and obtained a warrant for Thom's arrest. This was promptly issued and was entrusted to constable Nicholas Meares for execution.

As constable Meares approached him, Thom shot him dead. Then, after going into a neighbouring house asking 'Now am I not your Saviour?', he returned to the constable's body, fired a second pistol shot into it and started to hack it to pieces with his sword.

A major alert was mounted and one hundred men of the 45th Regiment of Foot, under Major Armstrong, were mobilised in support of the local constabulary. The force was split into two, under Lieutenants Bennett and Prendergast. They soon located Thom with his own 'army' of followers equipped with picks, forks and scythes. Armstrong called upon him to surrender, but Thom told his forty men to be of good cheer and to prepare for the battle.

He gave the order to charge, shooting Lieutenant Bennett dead. In a brief encounter, eight men were killed and many wounded. Lieutenant Prendergast was bludgeoned by an assailant and a constable was shot in the confusion.

Thom was felled by a truncheon, but rose – roaring – to his feet. Soon he was finally dead, killed by a musket ball fired by a soldier.

The full horror of the battle was brought home at the inquest. The wives, widows and children of Thom's followers were present, as were the wounded on stretchers. The bodies of the dead were laid out in a stable. During the hearing another two men died and were taken to the temporary mortuary. Lieutenant Bennett, it transpired, had actually been leaving the depot to go on holiday when the mobilisation began. He had immediately asked to go with his men.

The break-up of the fanatics had not come a day too soon. Before ordering his men into their fatal final action, Thom had promised them that, on the following Sunday, he would lead them to Canterbury where they would set fire to the city and have 'a glorious but a bloody day'.

BIRD'S EYE VIEW ... St Ives today – holiday beaches that were once the backdrop for treachery, conspiracy and murder.

BOOKS CONSULTED

Baring-Gould, Rev. Sabine, *Cornish Characters and Strange Events*, Bodley Head; Barton, D. Bradford, *Life in Cornwall*, D. Bradford Barton; Borlase, William, *Observation on the Isles of Scilly*, Frank Graham; Bowen, Frank, *His Majesty's Coastguard*, Hutchinson; Carson, Edward, *The Ancient and Rightful Customs*, Faber & Faber; *Chambers Biographical Dictionary*, Chambers; *Chambers Encyclopaedia*, Chambers; Cornish, John B., *A Cornish Smuggler*, Gibbings & Co.; Course, Captain A.G., *The Merchant Navy*, Muller; Coxe, Anthony D. Hippisley, *A Book About Smuggling in the Westcountry 1700-1850*, Tabb House; Dickens, Charles, *All The Year Round*, Chapman & Hall; Douch, H.L., *Old Cornish Inns*, D. Bradford Barton; Graham, Frank, *Cornwall 100 Years Ago*, Frank Graham; Halliday, F.E., *History of Cornwall*, Duckworth; Heath, Robert, *The Isles of Scilly*, Frank Graham; Jenkin, A.K. Hamilton, *Cornwall and its People*, David & Charles.

Mumford, Clive, *Portrait of the Isles of Scilly*, Robert Hale; Noall, Cyril, *Smuggling in Cornwall*, D. Bradford Barton; Pearce, John, *The Wesleys in Cornwall*, D. Bradford Barton; Pearse, Richard, *The Ports and Harbours of Cornwall*, H.E. Warne; Phillipson, David, *Smuggling – a history – 1700-1790*; Shore, Lieut. H.N., *Fighting Smuggling*; Shore, Lieut. H.N., *Smugglers of Fowey*; Shore, Lieut. H.N., *Smuggling Days and Smuggling Ways*, Cassell; Uren, J.G. *Scilly and the Scillonians*, Western Morning News; Vivian, John, *Tales of the Cornish Smugglers*, Tor Mark Press; Webb, William, *Coastguard!*, HMSO; Williams, Michael, *Curiosities of Cornwall*, Bossiney Books; Williams Michael, *Land's End*, Bossiney Books.

Files of: *The Gentleman's Magazine, Royal Cornwall Gazette, Sherborne Mercury, West Briton.*

LAND'S END ... Fickle sunlight glistens on the waves that tumble around some of the most famous cliffs in Britain. The only invaders now are the fishermen and trippers – but the more unorthodox ways of earning a living are still remembered wherever local people gather.